PRESENTATION DRAWINGS BY AMERICAN ARCHITECTS

Presentation Drawings By American Architects

ALFRED KEMPER, AIA

A WILEY-INTERSCIENCE PUBLICATION
JOHN WILEY & SONS   NEW YORK LONDON SYDNEY TORONTO

Library of Congress Cataloging in Publication Data

Main entry under title:

Presentation drawings by American architects.

"A Wiley-Interscience publication."
Includes indexes.
1. Architectural drawing.   2. Architectural rendering.   3. Architecture—Sketches.   4. Architecture—
Designs and plans.   5. Graphic arts—Technique.
6. Architects—United States.   I. Kemper, Alfred M.,
1933-

NA2700.P73   720'.28   76-40891
ISBN 0-471-01369-2

Printed in the United States of America

10 9 8 7 6 5 4 3

Foreword

Architectural presentation drawings serve two important purposes: first, to act as a tool for the architect in developing a design concept and, second, to communicate the architectural design to others.

As a design tool, presentation drawings are used by the architect to explore the design problem and to develop the solution. In an age of complexity and specialization the architect often functions as a member of a team composed of collaborators of diverse skills. Drawings serve as a common basis of communication between the team members. They provide a focus for evaluation and refinement. The drawing serves, not as an end in itself, but, more importantly, as a tool in an ongoing process. As such, the style and technique of the drawing may change throughout the process. Initially the drawings should be loose and sketchy, reflecting the early exploration in the conceptual phase. As the design solution becomes more clearly defined, the graphic representation becomes more detailed and refined. During the conceptual process an interaction occurs between the abstract idea and its visual realization. The concept may be modified as the design takes visual form. As the design evolves, graphics aid the architect in evaluating his work and refining the concept through detailing.

As a communication device the drawing explains the design to others. Traditionally the presentation drawing has been used mainly as a tool for selling the design. Unfortunately even a weak design solution can be made to "look" good. The client must use discerning judgment to evaluate the design, and the architect must not be deceived by his own artistry. If the client is viewed as a member of the design team, then the function of a graphic presentation is to present options, clearly allowing the client to make educated choices.

The purpose of a presentation drawing is an important determinant in how it is conceived and presented. The designer must consider who is being addressed, through what channel, and with what effect. In some cases the drawings must be able to stand completely alone, with no additional verbal explanation, but in others the drawings must complement an oral presentation.

Since the purpose of the drawing is to communicate information, anything that interferes with the clarity of the message should be eliminated. The viewer should get a clear picture of how the building works. The graphics can not only present the scheme but can also communicate its meaning with regard to organizational concepts (public versus private zones, functional clusters, primary versus secondary circulation, form response to specific environmental conditions, etc.). The graphics can communicate the three-dimensional ordering of the various elements of the building. This can occur at any point in the design process.

Thus graphics can involve the client in the evolution of the design. This reduces the gap between the architect, the client, and the user and reduces the risk of investing time and energy in a design that does not solve the problem.

As clients and users take a more active role in the design process and become more sophisticated, the emphasis will be on developing graphic techniques that will serve as a tool to test alternatives and aid the designer in translating the client's goals and needs into architecture.

High-quality graphic presentations not only communicate the architect's serious intentions to the client but also reinforce the dedication, discipline, and pride within the design team.

This book presents a diversity of examples of graphic techniques that an architect can employ.

Daniel L. Dworsky, FAIA

Preface

Presentation drawing may be described as the art of presenting a form by lines without reference to color. In general, presentation drawings are prepared by architects to show the client what his building (design) will look like. The designer often, however, produces various presentation drawings to satisfy his own curiosity and evaluate his design process. Before going into more detail on presentation (as such) I admit that in most cases the actual building may have an effect on the viewer that is completely different from the feeling he gets from viewing a presentation drawing.

The actual building is surrounded by atmospheric conditions, sun and wind, noise and odors, and, of course, color; all can stimulate moods that influence us psychologically and create a picture of realities far different from the drawn picture. A presentation drawing shows the building in a fixed view, a frozen stage. The drawing or "presentation" should, therefore, be admired for the sake of its presentation and for the play of lines. For this reason I have left out all reference to the actual design, both the name and the type of project.

What matters primarily is the architect and the renderer. The name of the architect or of his office is shown at the right bottom of the drawing, and that of the renderer at the left bottom. If only one name is shown, then the architect is also the renderer or vice versa.

This book is divided into 20 sections, each representing a unique part of the process of presenting a design phase. All previous books on renderings show buildings in perspective only, including the book **Drawings by American Architects**, which I edited a few years ago (same publisher). This is the first book on the market to show the complete range of presentation phases, such as plans, elevations, and sections, that are produced to complete the design, from conceptual sketches to schematics, to plans, to elevations, to the final perspective showing the overall picture.

The purpose of this book is to show the many different presentation techniques used for drawing by various American architects across the country, many of which were submitted for the earlier book. The drawings were executed in and/or for the office both to study and design the project, as well as to be presented to the client, an art commission, or the like. Because this book was produced specifically for our profession, it is divided into sections by the various types of drawings rather than by offices. Thus it will be helpful to architects as a reference tool in respect to type of drawing and/or technique. Regardless of the size of the firm, the type of drawing used is the same, depending on the desired effect.

I remind the reader that the selection of drawings does not include all the offices in the United States; those not represented here were unable to meet the deadline for publication. Moreover, the number of drawings per architect indicates neither the size nor the activity of his office but merely the extent of my personal contact with his office.

Also omitted are any references to the history of drawings or to the past masters, since a number of books are available on these topics. I am, however, thankful to the office of Shepley Bulfinch Richardson & Abbott for letting me reproduce a short "American" history of drawings.

To provide equal credit and ease of reference, an index of offices and an index of renderers are supplied. For any changes in the names of offices, owing to merging, disassociation, relocation, or other cause, please contact the American Institute of Architects in Washington, D.C.

Should any drawing, office, or renderer be misidentified, please inform the publisher and I shall personally thank you.

In the book **Drawings by American Architects** I expressed my hope that the collection of drawings would help the client understand the different ways of presenting architecture. I still hope that the book will serve this function in the future. I hope that this book will help architects, designers, and engineers learn from each other the importance of the various techniques used to present various design phases.

I express my deep appreciation and sincere thanks to the many architects who submitted drawings for both books in the true spirit of fellowship advocated by all members of the AIA to help each other in the higher interests of our profession.

Alfred M. Kemper, AIA
Los Angeles, California
November 1976

Contents

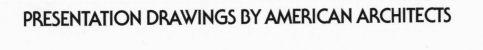

PRESENTATION DRAWINGS BY AMERICAN ARCHITECTS

Introduction

The architect sketches primarily to test his conceptual ideas, redo or refine them, and afterward submit them to others by means of a "presentation" or final drawing. This requires both mental exercise and physical discipline. Sketching is often dismissed as an innate gift of coordination of the hand and as something incapable of being learned (or taught), but this is not so. In my opinion drawing demands much more intellect than skill of hand; drawing in itself is pure design, but it is not the end to design. I hope this book will persuade the reader either to start drawing or to continue to draw and try all kinds of methods, systems, and ways until he or she finds his or her own way of presenting a drawing.

The difference between working drawings and architectural presentation is generally known. Whereas the first is used only to instruct someone how to construct the building, architectural presentation is used for a variety of reasons. The designer uses it during the design process; he uses it also for showing to fellow architects (at competitions), art committees, and others, but mostly he uses it to demonstrate to the client how his building will appear. Hence, architectural presentations are drawings stripped of any entourage, so that one may see clearly what is important to the designer of the building (or to the client).

In architectural practice four basic drawings have been established for presenting and constructing a building: the plan (also plot plan), elevation, section, and perspective. They are generally put in this order of importance for the following reasons: the plan shows the size of the building and its function, the elevation shows its height and general appearance, the section shows the height of the interior and also the manner in which it is constructed, and the perspective, though not used as frequently, is mostly employed to sell the "idea" to the client and even to the designer himself. Depending on the building, however, this sequence of importance is not rigidly set, because some concepts exist more strongly in section, some in plan, and so forth. In a way though, all design aspects do exist in perspective, and ultimately the building's life is lived three-dimensionally and thus totally in perspective. A good designer uses the perspective constantly in design, especially the partial perspective, but the other three drawings communicate his idea in far more detail than the perspective does. The perspective shows everything in one overall view, in one glance. But the client wants to see all sides of the building, its interior, and also some details. The architect must, therefore, master all techniques and means to help communicate his concepts to others.

Only two basic presentation techniques are used in architecture: line or tone. All other techniques, including the use of color, are derived from these two by

1

combination or by variations within one or the other. But technique is not the only requisite in architectural presentation. It is also important to know the materials to be used and to know how to suggest landscaping, trees, people, shadows, and so forth. These must be presented realistically and yet be graphically simple enough for the chosen technique. Let us briefly discuss some of these aspects.

LINE DRAWINGS

The line drawing delineates surfaces and plane intersections by the outlines. Basically an abstraction, it shows the edges (lines) formed between contrasting tones (surfaces or planes). Most line drawings also indicate texture by the use of the line.

One of the most widely used techniques among architects, the line drawing is also the best devised for drawing buildings because these are not amorphous. All construction drawings are of course drawn in line. The line drawing is very flexible; it can be "filled in" with tone, colors, and unlimited texture variations. The essence of the line drawing is its continuity. It must show a continuous stroke. This skill (or confidence) can be acquired only by much practice, even by first drawing a very fine line and then correcting it with a heavier line afterward. In a pure line drawing the variation in the weight (thickness) of the line is the only means of expression. This can be achieved either by drawing various thin lines close together to achieve a thick line or by using various pencil or pen sizes. The greater the variation in line weight, the clearer the drawing, provided there is a discernible meaning behind the line variations, for the idea behind architectural presentation is showing space, and this can be achieved only by assigning line weight values within the drawing technique. Line drawings are the most efficient way to draw and therefore the least expensive to reproduce. They require one simple tool, either a pencil or a pen of any kind. They describe forms and spaces precisely with an absolute minimum of effort and time. The single line is used in our written language to make definite separations and designs and may express a variety of functions. These same ideas are incorporated when the working drawing is ultimately used as a pattern for the building to be constructed.

Excellent examples of line drawings are produced, in my opinion, by the architects Paul Rudolph and William Kirby Lockard. A book is available showing all of Paul Rudolph's drawings. Paul Rudolph also wrote the introduction to the first book I edited, **Drawings by American Architects.** William Kirby Lockard, professor at the University of Arizona, wrote an excellent book on drawings. Other excellent examples in this book are by the office of Venturi & Rauch.

TONE DRAWINGS

The tone drawing depends on the contrast between one tone and another to indicate surfaces or planes. Edges of planar intersections are designated by changes in tone value. This type of drawing is the most realistic, for it resembles the way we perceive things in reality. In other words it is the least abstract. In the tone drawing the line profiling an object becomes the meeting line of two different tone values. To establish this meeting line requires extensive training, much more so than the line drawing. This meeting line is not as important within the total frame of the picture as the medium line in a line drawing. For instance the tonal difference between a floor surface and a wall at their intersection may not be the same as that between a shadow and a shaded area.

All tone drawings are reproduced by the half-tone process, in which a screen is placed over the original drawing. This changes the tones to relatively dense areas of tiny dots. Even a line reproduced in this way is printed as a line of dots, and from this fact arises the soft quality of this type of drawing.

LINE-TONE (VARIATION) TECHNIQUE

In principle the line–tone technique is a tone drawing. The difference lies in the fact that the tones (surfaces) are made of lines. The relative values of the tones are achieved by the various spacings of the lines. The ends of all lines are the meeting lines of the surfaces (tones). Therefore, the difference of the line weight is not as important in a line–tone technique as in a simple line drawing. The space between the lines and also the directions of the lines become the main aspect of this technique. In general, floors, ceilings, and other horizontal surfaces should be shown with lines running across the picture, from side to side. Walls and other vertical surfaces should correspondingly be indicated with vertical lines. The line-tone technique is the best technique for reduction as well as reproduction.

The architect H. Jacoby has used this technique to perfection, and so has Carlos Diniz. This book shows several samples of various types. H. Jacoby has published several books showing his own drawings. Other well-known architects are John Desmond, Ted Kantzky, Hugh Ferriss, Davis Bite, and, of course, Steve Oles. I have provided a special section for Steve Oles in this book.

LINE AND TONE (COMBINATION) TECHNIQUE

Since this is a combination technique, both line and tone techniques lose a bit of their characteristics. For instance the commitment to various line thicknesses becomes less important, and consequently the tone value differentiation becomes less significant, for the line replaces the meeting line previously discussed. In fact the line may also be used to indicate a surface and thus combine tone and line for the subject surface. The best known tone used in this technique is the so-called Zip-A-Tone (or other manufactured products). Textured tones as well as pencil tones or ink washes are used, all in combination with line work of various thicknesses, drawn either precisely or freehand. The most famous architect using this technique is Gordon Cullen, from England. His book **Townscape** shows numerous samples. Excellent examples in this book are by the designer Craig Elwood.

DESIGN FEATURES

LIGHT AND SHADOW Light is as much a part of architecture as material or space is. During designing the architect should habitually evaluate the light of the space and draw and study the shaded surfaces and cast shadows. Even in the smallest sketches, shades and shadows should be dominant. The layman recognizes the language of light without special training because we live in a world of light shades and shadows. Whether it is in a plan, elevation, or section, any viewer can read the third dimension created by the shadow system, although he is unable to project it himself. Numerous books are available on light and shadow that explain the projecting (casting) of shadows by any source of light, whether by artificial light or sunlight. This is a very important field of study for an architect, and once mastered, it is a useful tool for the architect that will prevent the careless presentation that misleads both designer and client. Too often shadows are used only as a presentation device and surfaces are shown in vibrant sunlight when in reality they will be in shade or overcast by a deep shadow.

In architectural presentation there is room for experiment with the light's angle and direction to find a shadow situation that best communicates the architecture. But the architect must exercise responsibility so that this situation is not the exception, such as a condition that occurs only at 7 A.M. on the second of January or, in the case of artificial light, the condition when only one side of the room (space) is lighted. Interior spaces are in general more difficult to present,

3

since the light level is more diffused. A general rule is that surfaces facing the light (or normal to this light source) are the brightest and surfaces backing the light source are darkest. Surfaces parallel to the direction of the light source are shaded in various tones, depending on their distance from the light source.

In general, shadows in architectural presentation are cast on a 45-degree angle, in plan, elevation, or section. All shadows are cast by the line that separates sunlight and shade. Shadows give a third (true) dimension to a drawing, even though in reality the shadow moves according to the position of the light source.

LETTERING Traditionally architects are good letterers, for lettering is an important part of working drawings. Our alphabets have been refined throughout the centuries, and it is difficult to improve on the lettering styles used in architectural presentation, with the exception of those used and placed on the building itself. Part of the design process is to select and/or create and place lettering on the building. For architectural presentation many excellent reference collections of alphabets and typefaces are available. Most are available as rub-ons, in templet form, or on traceable sheets to any scale desired.

MATERIALS In construction drawings various symbols are used that indicate the type of materials; all symbols have to do with communicating how a building is to be built. Presentation drawings show only how the building will look. For this reason a completely new set of graphic symbols is used to indicate materials in architectural presentation, although some symbols from the construction drawings are used in an abstract way in presentation drawings, such as the symbol for a door swing, directional arrows, and dimensions.

In addition to showing the texture of the material (and at times the color) one should also indicate the physical size of the material or the character of the unit. This means that, in woodsiding, individual boards or panels must be delineated, and in a masonry building the individual stones must be shown.

Today's materials are a bit harder to draw, because their surface textures are very similar. Aluminum, stainless steel, glass, formica, and many of the various maintenance-free materials are almost impossible to make distinguishable in simple line drawings. Often graphic symbols employed for ground cover will be confusing if used for vertical surfaces and vice versa. The symbol for exposed aggregate on vertical surfaces may easily be confused for gravel on a horizontal plane. Material indications should be clear and concise and indicate the textural character as well as the particular unit size without overpowering the building.

LANDSCAPING Architectural plans have always included the site plan, the area around the building. Today the transitional space of the urban site is very important, not only for the building itself, but also for the function of the interior of the building in relation to its total environment. There are many ways to indicate the soft areas in a plan. As with any of the other symbols, the ground indication may range from the specific to the very abstract, depending on the degree of accuracy needed.

The important thing to remember is to choose symbols consistent with the architecture, the climate, and the entourage used.

THE FIGURE The human figure is a graphic symbol used by many architects, not only to enliven the drawing, but also primarily to give scale to the building or space. The viewer can instantly feel the size of the building and orient himself within the proposed space. More so than with trees there are many personal styles or means of drawing people. However, as with trees in an elevation or a section, figures may range from the very abstract to the elaborately realistic. These figures may indicate specific characteristics as well as the activities of the persons within the building design, such as that of the doorman. Again the background determines the type of figure used as well as the scale of the drawing.

TREES A tree in a plan is the graphic detail most frequently used by architects. There are as many personal styles or ways of showing trees as there are architects (or designers). These may range from a simple circle to the most sophisticated form showing the entire trunk structure and all its branches and foliage. Showing a good tree depends not only on the scale in which it is drawn but also on the overall composition of the sheet, as well as the type of tree being represented. There are countless possibilities for gaining a familiar picture of a tree in a plan.

In an elevation or a section the shape of the tree, the structure of the branches, the thickness, the species, and even the season of the year can be shown with much greater accuracy than in a plan. In an elevation the tree can be shown impressionistically or realistically, with texture and shadow indication. This also depends on the type of drawing it is used for and the scale to which it is drawn.

VEHICLES Vehicles in a drawing are used primarily to designate the space and its usage. But they also provide a reference to scale and enliven the drawing. Any graphic symbolism indicating vehicles should not promote any specific type, unless it is especially called for. The prime significance is to show the dimensions of the space in relationship to the vehicle. This is particularly true of commercial vehicles such as buses, trucks, airplanes, and boats.

5

FURNITURE Drawing furniture (or fixtures) such as bathtubs, sinks, beds, tables, rows of seating, or bleachers clearly indicates the purpose of a specific room. Furniture is a directly communicative item to the eyes of the viewer that helps him judge the size of a room or space. It also documents the type of building, whether it be residential, multipurpose, industrial, or commercial.

MISCELLANEOUS DETAILS Many of the drawings produced by architects tend to be empty abstractions of forms; graphic details are often overlooked. A poor design cannot always be improved upon, even with the implementation of a skillful ability with graphic details. A drawing may, however, gain clarity with the intelligent employment of good symbols. The geographical surroundings of a structure may be indicated with the proper use of symbols such as trees and vehicles. These symbols not only animate the drawing but also give scale and proportion to the building. In the same way symbols in the interior of a building may show the intended activities as well as the proportions of the interior space.

GRAPHIC SYMBOLS The north arrow provides a purely objective item of information indicating the direction and orientation of the building plan in relation to the sun. Linear scales are used mainly to help the viewer of the drawing evaluate dimensions on the building. With certain limits scales lend themselves to graphic modifications.

Sketches

1

The first drawings an architect does are sketches, which may vary from mere doodles on the back of an envelope, to travel sketches, to very fine concept sketches. In my own opinion sketching is the most exciting stage of the design of a building. Sketches represent the language of thoughts, ideas, and imagination. No drawing stage truly represents the desired architecture, but of the concepts the architect's mind develops, the sketch probably comes closest. During the process of refining the sketches the truly imagined architecture usually gets lost.

The sketches in this section were selected from a limited number of individuals, because most offices, for one reason or another, are reluctant to release concept sketches. The most famous sketches are probably those by the late E. Mendelsohn. With just a few strokes the sketch readily identifies the main characteristics of the building. There were other "masters" whose sketches became famous, all published in books about the individual master.

Most sketches, in the true sense of sketching, are usually not good enough for a client or layman to understand and visualize or appreciate. For this reason I have selected sketches that would be accepted by a layman–client. Sketching is something of a lost art, and since the major part of architecture is becoming a technical service, only a few of us produce sketches during the design stages to record an idea or thought process or to review or modify this idea. For this reason sketches are very private and tentative. This is why freedom of technique is imperative.

8

WALTER GREUB

GERALD K. LEE

ESHERICK, HOMSEY, DODGE, AND DAVIS **9**

FRED LAPPIN

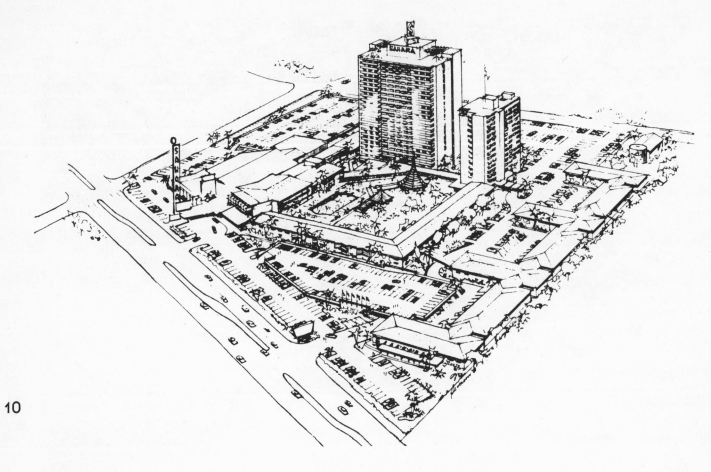

10

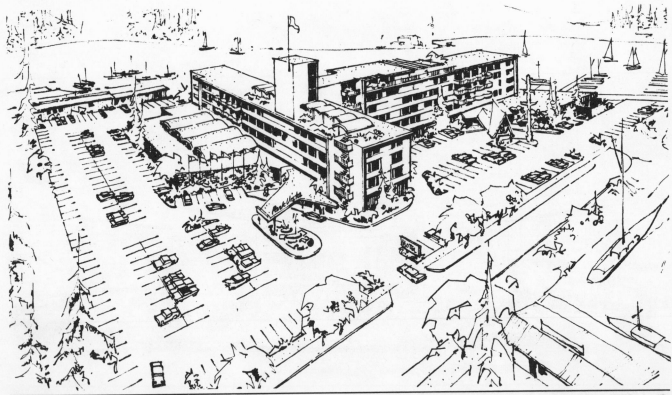

BERTON CHARLES SEVERSON   MARTIN STERN, JR.

ROMALDO GIURGOLA   MITCHELL/GIURGOLA ASSOCIATES

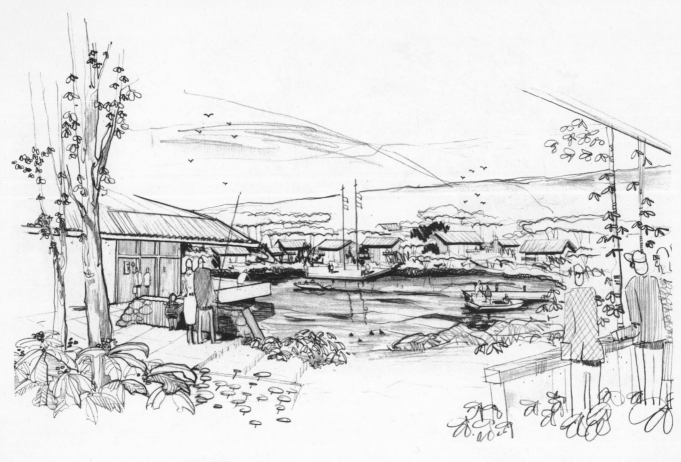

12

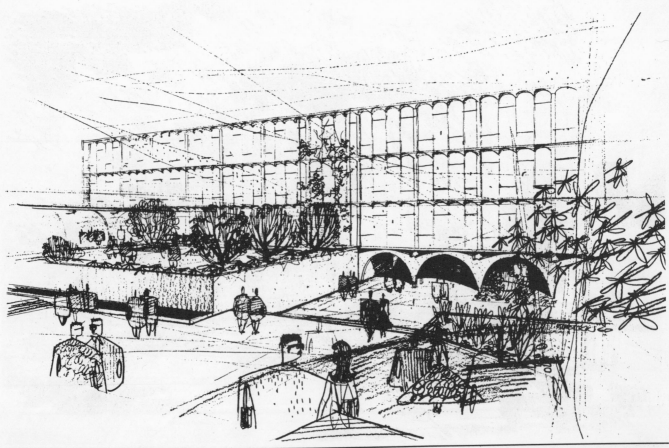

GEORGE VERNON RUSSELL

LEAVITT DUDLEY

DANIEL, MANN, JOHNSON, AND MENDENHALL

H. M. PAYNE JR.

TAC

14

JOHN DESMOND

HIKO TAKEDA

ERNEST J. KUMP ASSOCIATES

16

JOHN JOHANSEN

Bertrand Goldberg Associates

Marina City Detroit

A. GOERS

BERTRAND GOLDBERG ASSOCIATES

18 THOMAS AIDALA   DEMARS AND WELLS

TAD LESKI   HARRISON AND ABRAMOVITZ

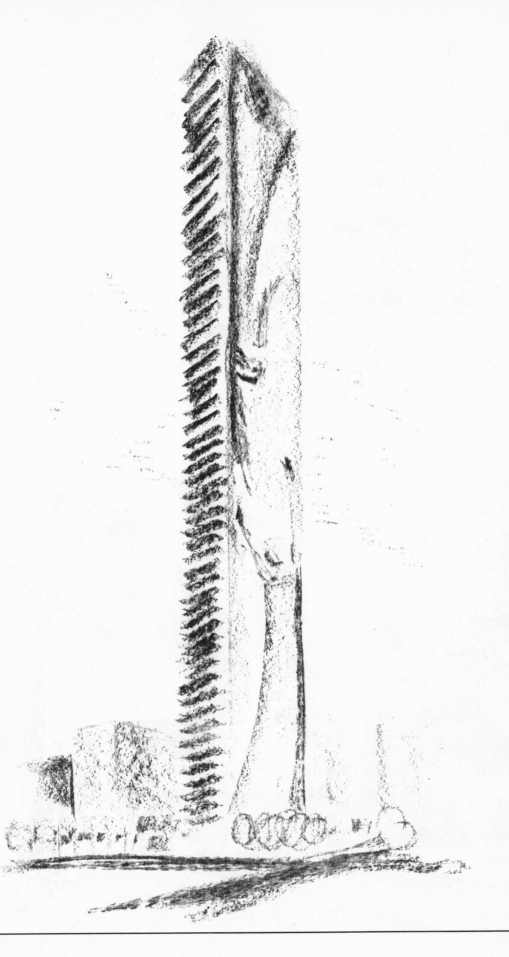

19

A. M. KEMPER

22

23

R. SUTHERLAND

WALLACE, McHARG, ROBERTS, AND TODD

Florence '65 ms

Notre Dame Paris
'65 rms

rms '65

R. SUTHERLAND WALLACE, McHARG, ROBERTS, AND TODD

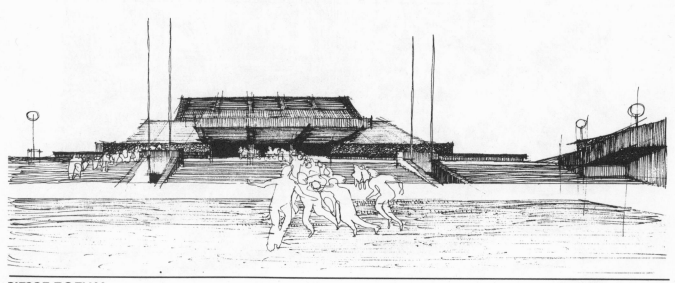

PIERRE ZOELLY

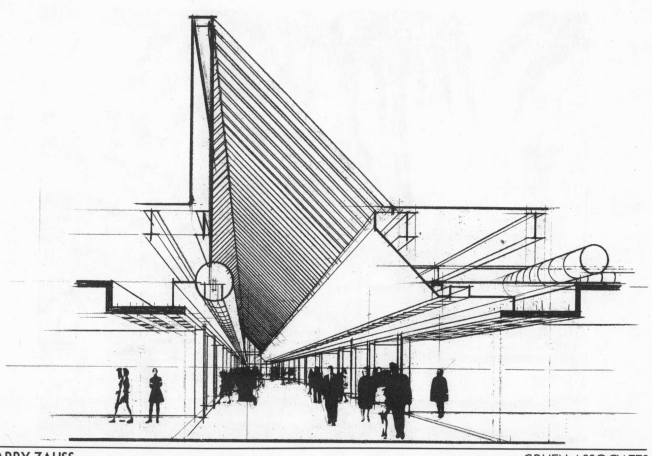

BARRY ZAUSS

GRUEN ASSOCIATES

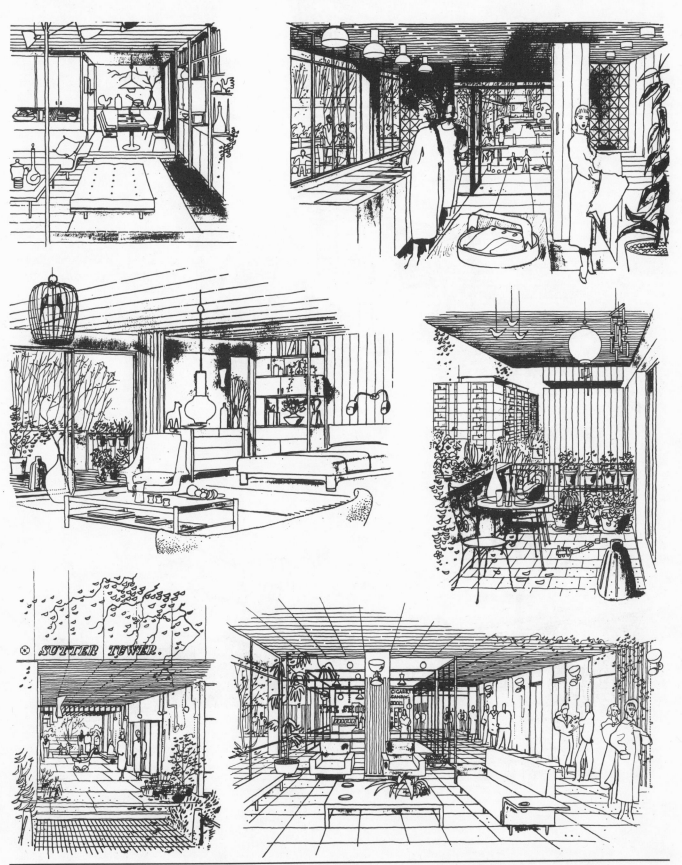

27

WURSTER, BERNARDI, AND EMMONS, INC.

28

JOHN C. MAYERS

JAMES BISCHOFF

CHRISTOPHER RIDDLE

CALLISTER AND PAYNE

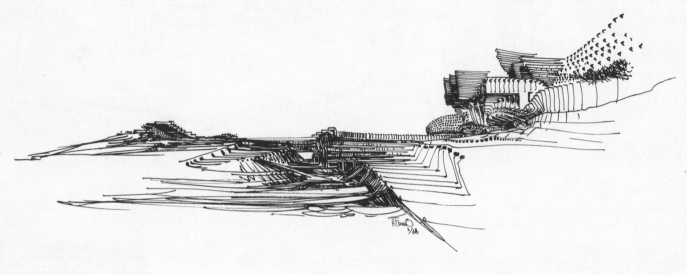

30

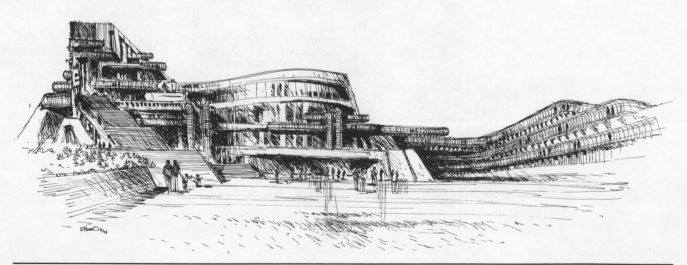

H. FERRERO

H. FERRERO

FERRERO-WITKOWSKI

32

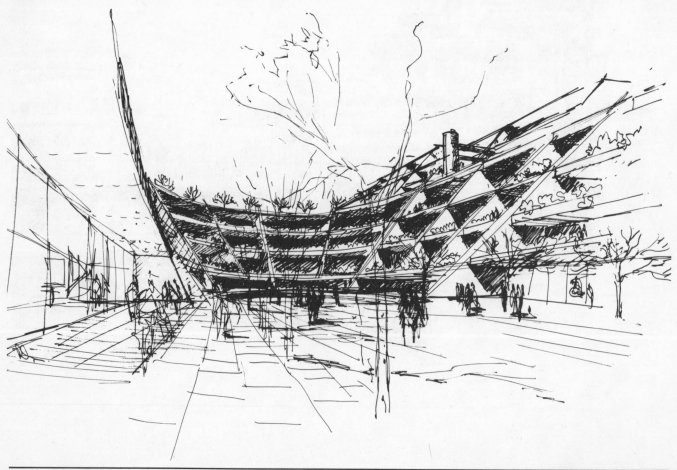

CARLOS DINIZ   HONNOLD, REIBSAMEN, AND REX

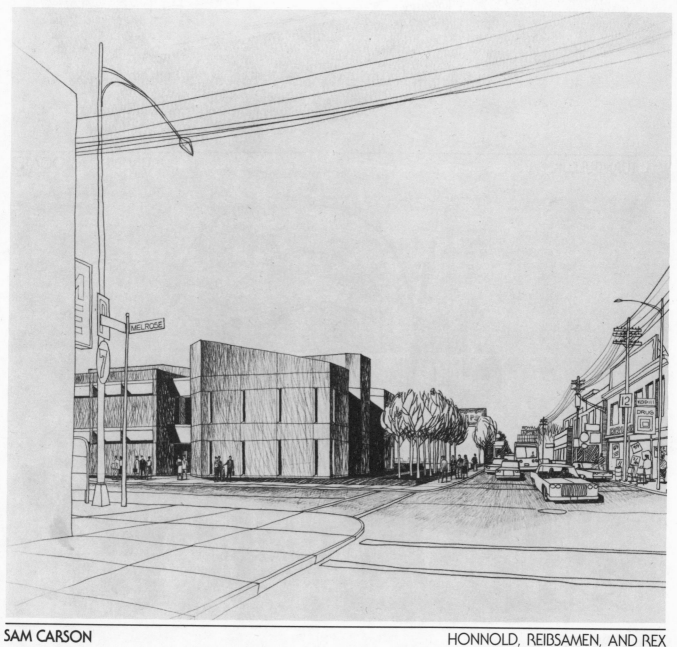

SAM CARSON

HONNOLD, REIBSAMEN, AND REX

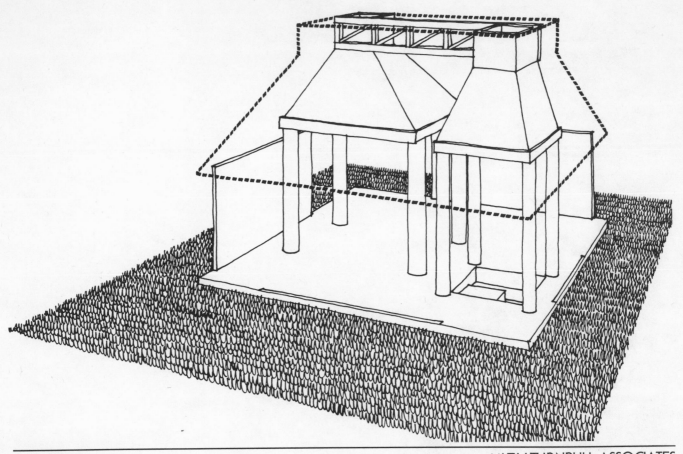

MLTW/TURNBULL ASSOCIATES

CHARLES WARNER, JR.

HARLAN GEORGESCO

36 CHARLES WARNER, JR.

MELVIN AMINOFF   WARNER, BURNS, TOAN, LUNDE

JAMES K. M. CHENG   BULL, FIELD, VOLKMANN, STOCKWELL

Plot Plans

2

Plot or site plans are one of the first finalized drawings produced by the architect. Although the final site plan is worked out with outside consultants, such as landscape architects, civil engineers, or parking consultants, the architect is responsible for presenting to the client a finished drawing. The main purpose of a plot plan is to show the position of a building relative to its surroundings. The following examples show a variety of ways to present a plot plan.

38

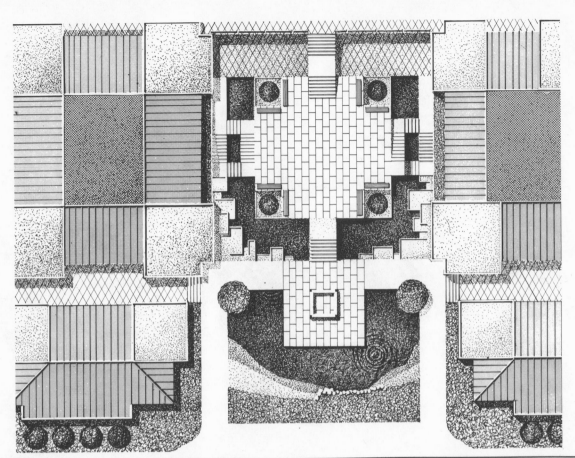

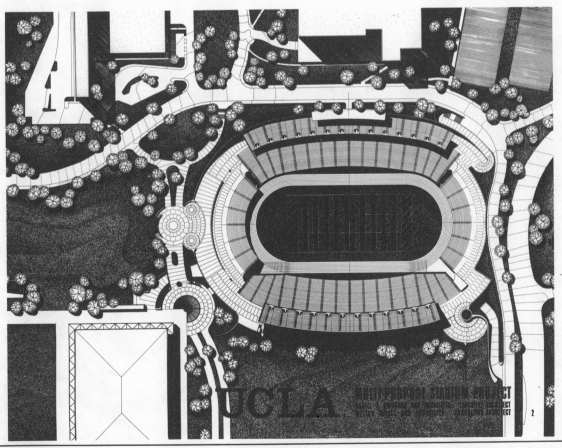

DAN DWORSKY

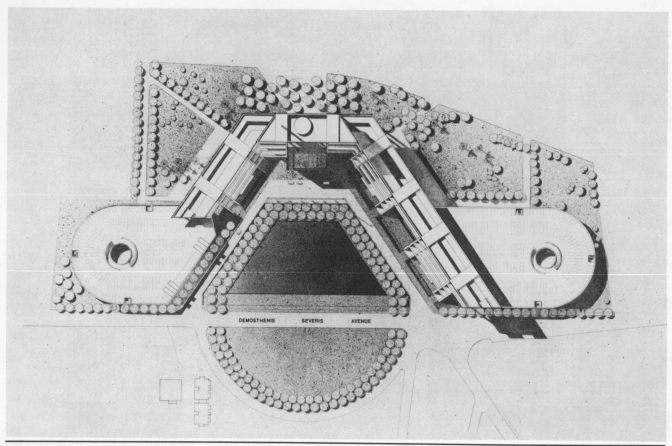

DEMOSTHENIS · SEVERIS · AVENUE

40 T. N. LARSON AND J. SHEEHY   TAC

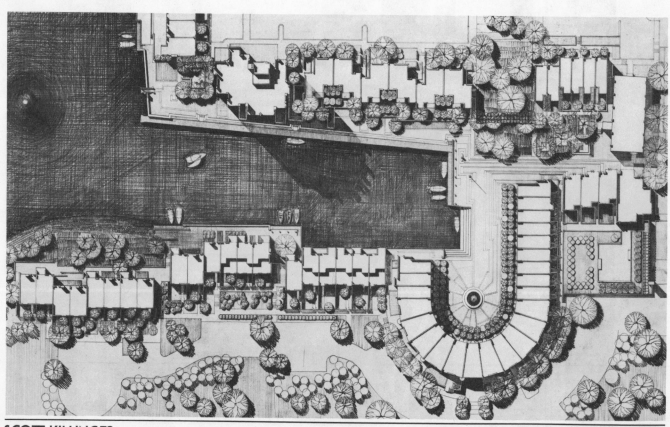

SCOTT KILLINGER   CONKLIN & ROSSANT

BUSCH CT.

MARVIN HATAMI

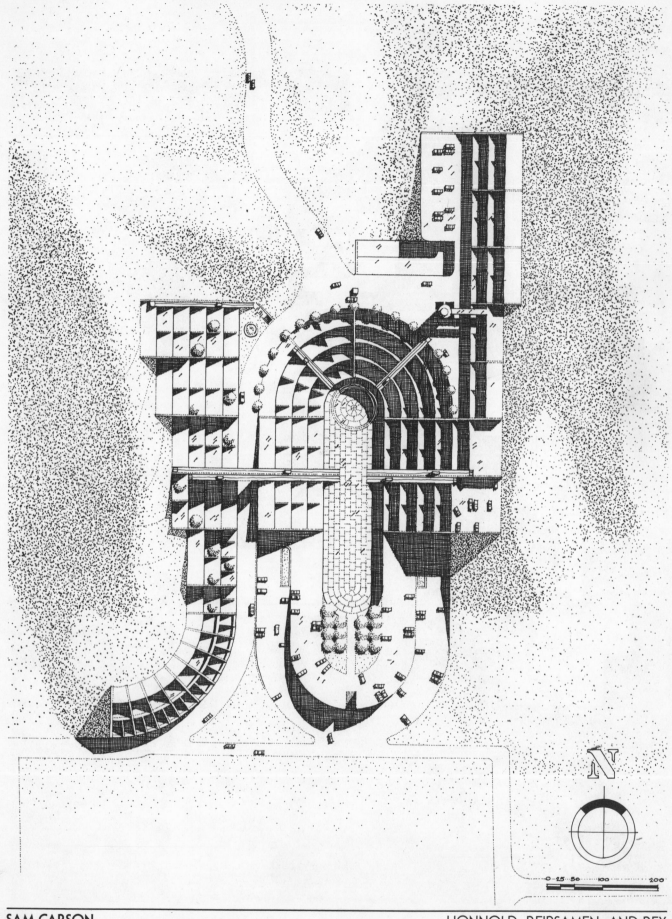

42

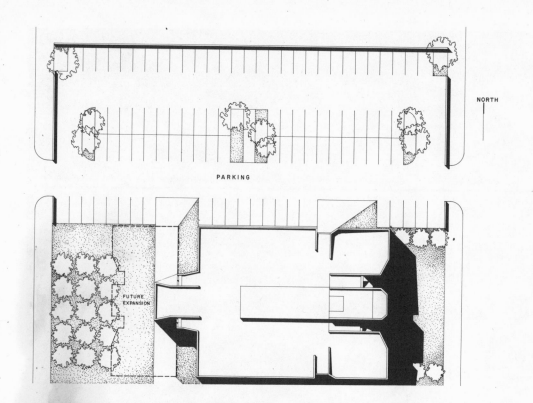

NORTH

PARKING

FUTURE
EXPANSION

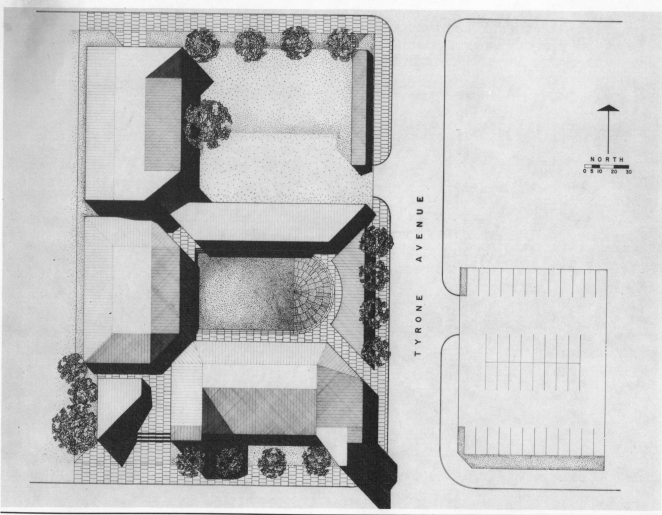

43

NORTH
0 5 10   20   30

TYRONE AVENUE

SAM CARSON

HONNOLD, REIBSAMEN, AND REX

44

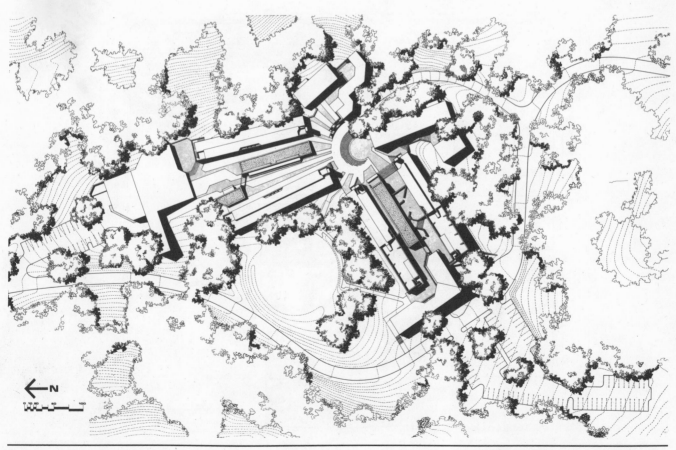

N

MLTW/TURNBULL ASSOCIATES

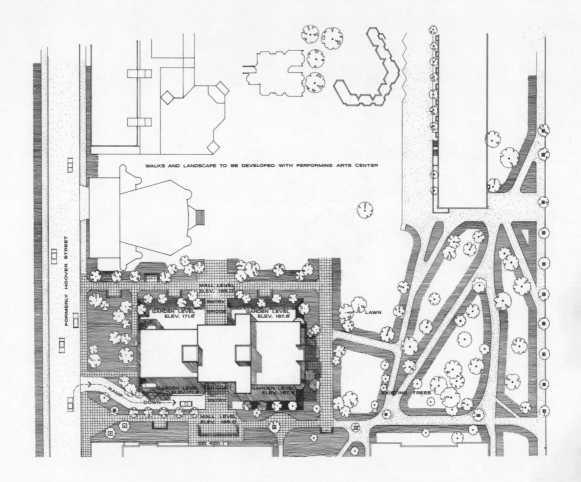

WALKS AND LANDSCAPE TO BE DEVELOPED WITH PERFORMING ARTS CENTER

FORMERLY HOOVER STREET

MALL LEVEL

GARDEN LEVEL
ELEV. 171.6'

GARDEN LEVEL
ELEV. 167.6'

LAWN

BRIDGE

GARDEN LEVEL
ELEV. 171.6'

BRIDGE
ENTRY

GARDEN LEVEL
ELEV. 167.6'

RAMP
DOWN

MALL LEVEL

EXISTING TREES

46

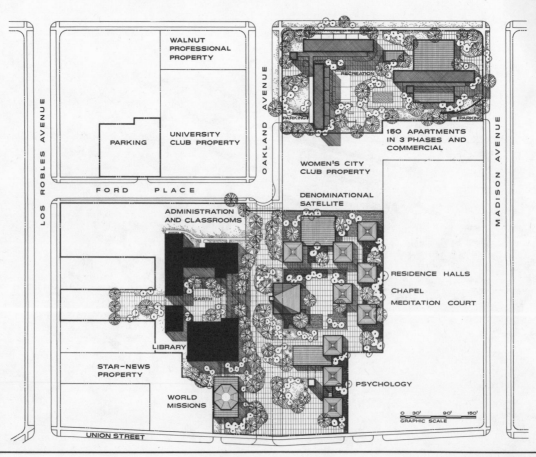

LOS ROBLES AVENUE

WALNUT
PROFESSIONAL
PROPERTY

PARKING

UNIVERSITY
CLUB PROPERTY

FORD PLACE

OAKLAND AVENUE

RECREATION

PARKING

PARKING

150 APARTMENTS
IN 3 PHASES AND
COMMERCIAL

MADISON AVENUE

WOMEN'S CITY
CLUB PROPERTY

DENOMINATIONAL
SATELLITE

ADMINISTRATION
AND CLASSROOMS

RESIDENCE HALLS

CHAPEL

MEDITATION COURT

GARTH

LIBRARY

STAR-NEWS
PROPERTY

WORLD
MISSIONS

PSYCHOLOGY

0 30'   90'   150'
GRAPHIC SCALE

UNION STREET

A. QUINCY JONES

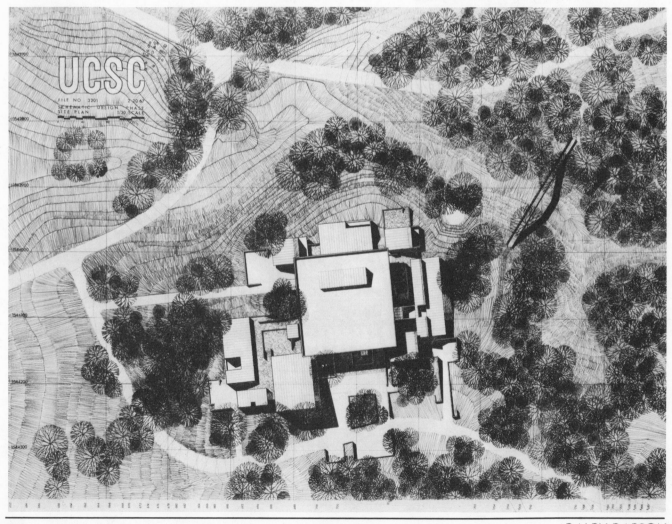

RALPH RAPSON

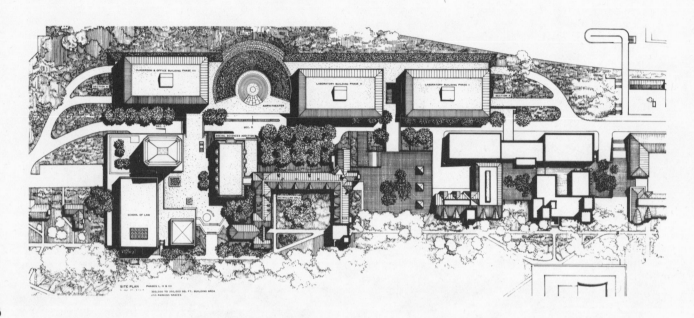

SITE PLAN   PHASES I, II & III
300,000 TO 350,000 SQ. FT. BUILDING AREA
310 PARKING SPACES

48

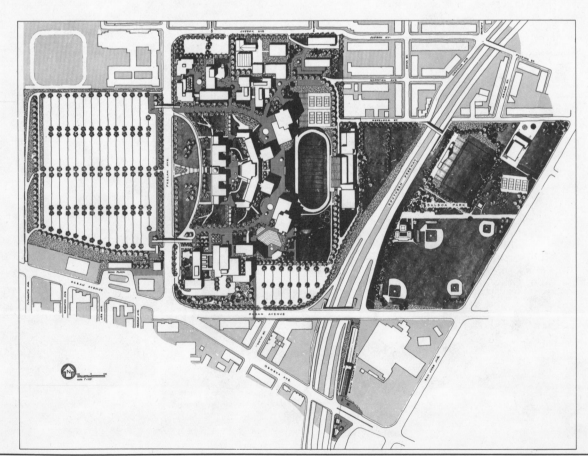

JACK SAGEN   MILTON T. PFLUEGER

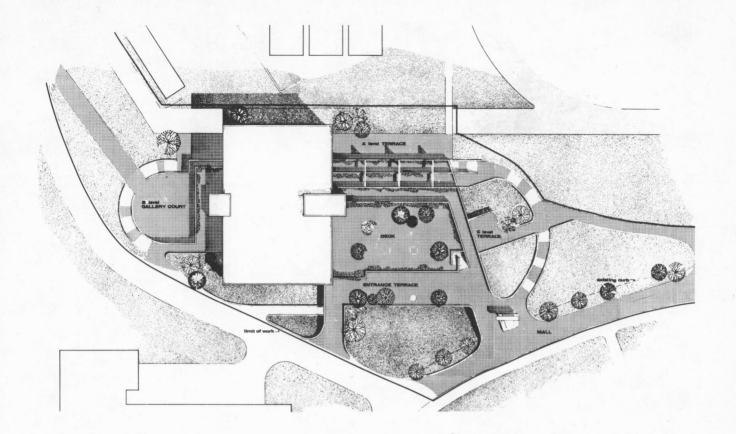

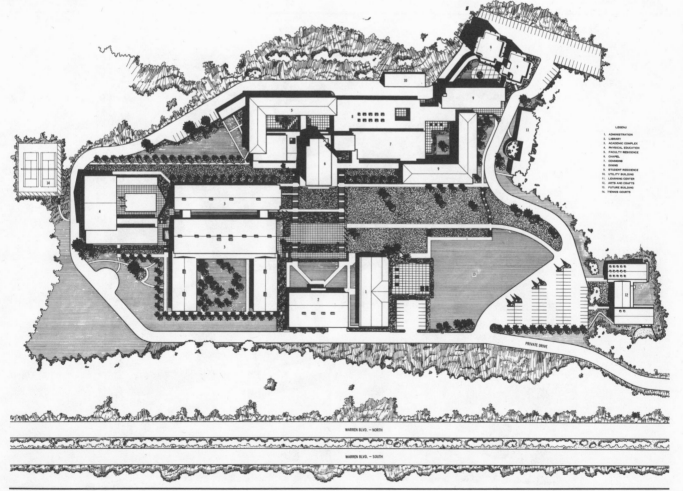

LEGEND

1. ADMINISTRATION
2. LIBRARY
3. ACADEMIC COMPLEX
4. PHYSICAL EDUCATION
5. FACULTY RESIDENCE
6. CHAPEL
7. COMMONS
8. DINING
9. STUDENT RESIDENCE
10. UTILITY BUILDING
11. LEARNING CENTER
12. ARTS AND CRAFTS
13. FUTURE BUILDING
14. TENNIS COURTS

JACK SAGEN   **MILTON T. PFLUEGER**

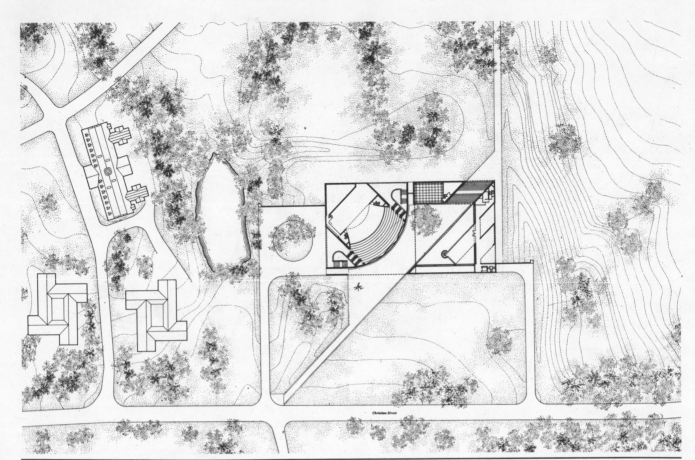

I. M. PEI AND PARTNERS

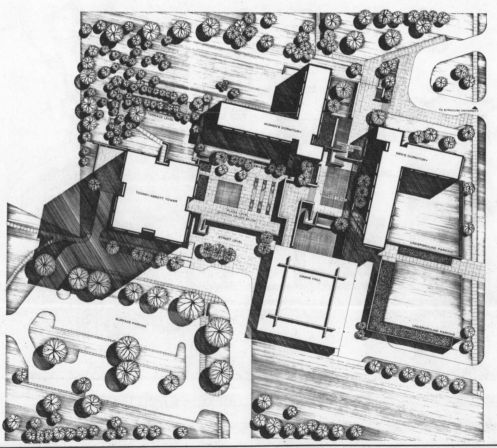

SARGENT, WEBSTER, CRENSHAW, AND FOLLEY

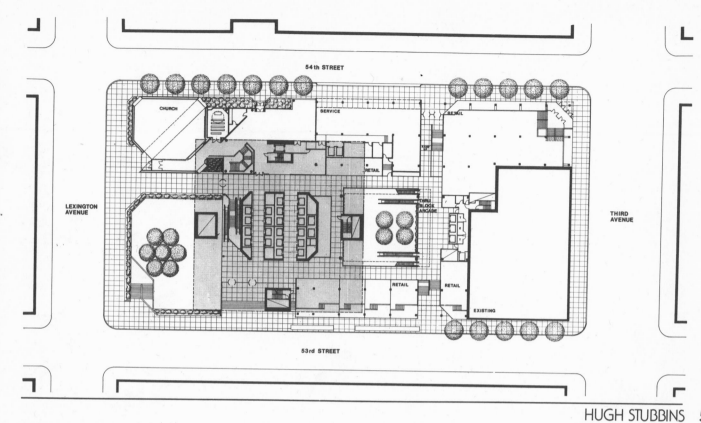

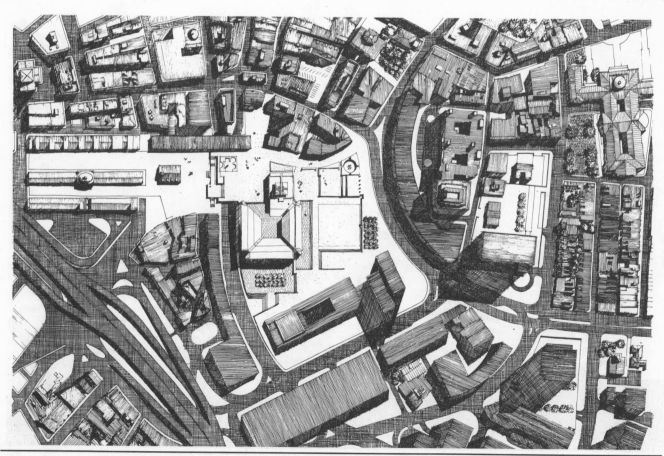

MITCHELL/GIURGOLA ASSOCIATES

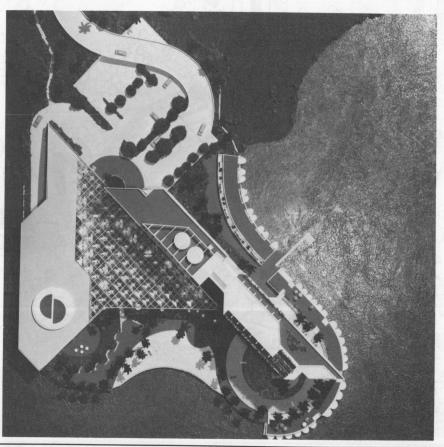

BOB RANDALL (MODEL SHOP)   TAC

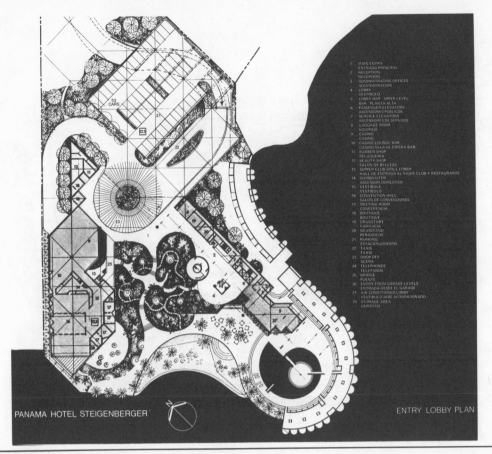

PANAMA HOTEL STEIGENBERGER   ENTRY LOBBY PLAN

COLBERT ANDRUS   TAC 55

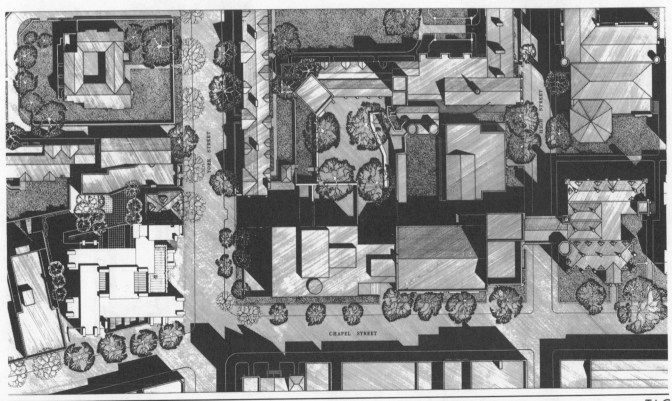

MICHAEL GEBHART   TAC

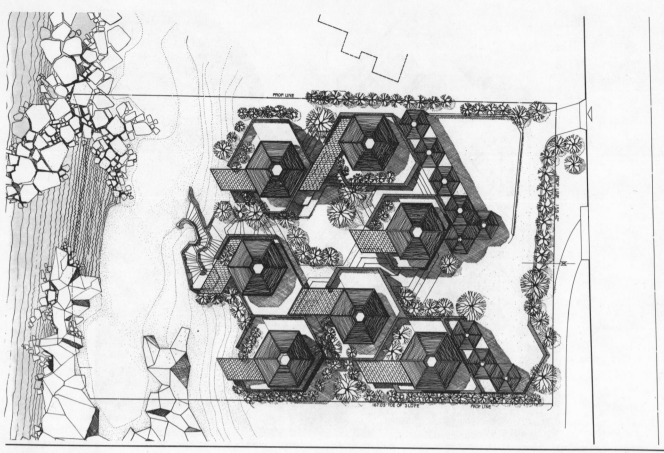

56

CARL MASTON

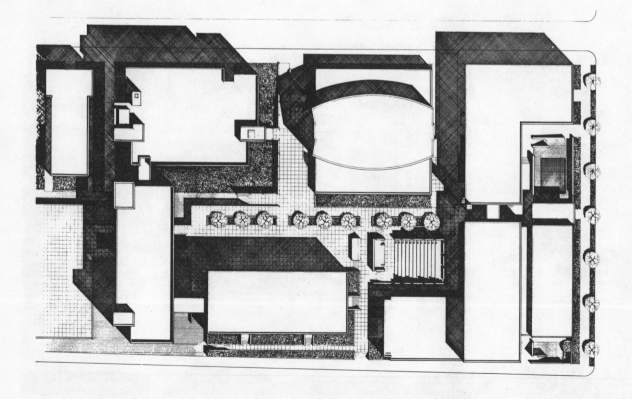

JOHN H. CROWTHER

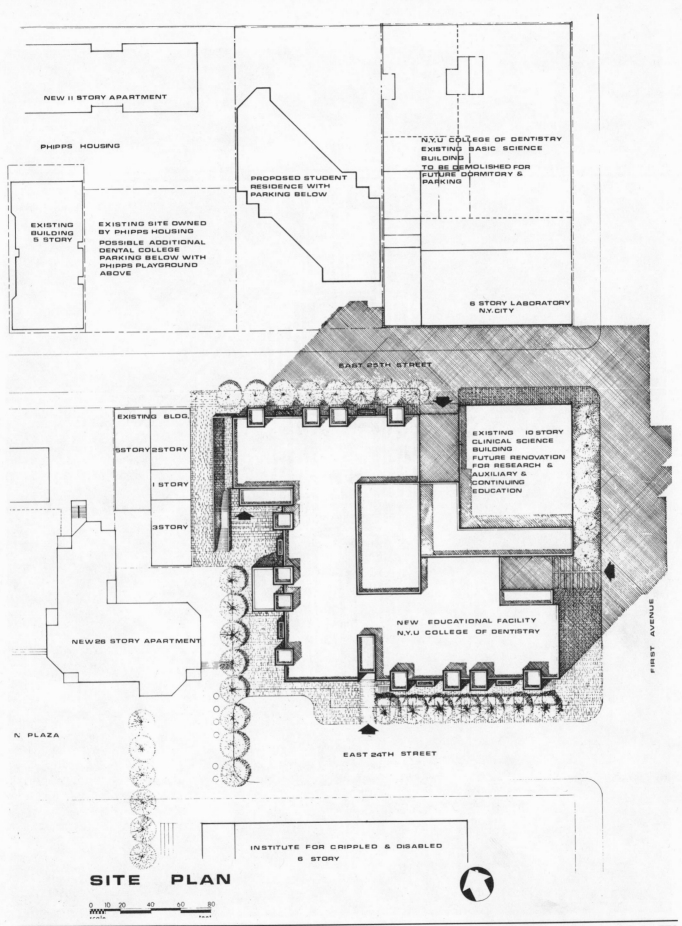

NEW 11 STORY APARTMENT

PHIPPS HOUSING

EXISTING
BUILDING
5 STORY

EXISTING SITE OWNED
BY PHIPPS HOUSING

POSSIBLE ADDITIONAL
DENTAL COLLEGE
PARKING BELOW WITH
PHIPPS PLAYGROUND
ABOVE

PROPOSED STUDENT
RESIDENCE WITH
PARKING BELOW

N.Y.U COLLEGE OF DENTISTRY
EXISTING BASIC SCIENCE
BUILDING
TO BE DEMOLISHED FOR
FUTURE DORMITORY &
PARKING

6 STORY LABORATORY
N.Y.CITY

EAST 25TH STREET

EXISTING BLDG.

5 STORY   2 STORY

1 STORY

3 STORY

EXISTING   10 STORY
CLINICAL SCIENCE
BUILDING
FUTURE RENOVATION
FOR RESEARCH &
AUXILIARY &
CONTINUING
EDUCATION

57

NEW 26 STORY APARTMENT

NEW EDUCATIONAL FACILITY
N.Y.U COLLEGE OF DENTISTRY

FIRST AVENUE

N PLAZA

EAST 24TH STREET

INSTITUTE FOR CRIPPLED & DISABLED
6 STORY

SITE   PLAN

0 10 20   40   60   80
scale   feet

CHARLES REDMON

CAMBRIDGE SEVEN ASSOCIATES

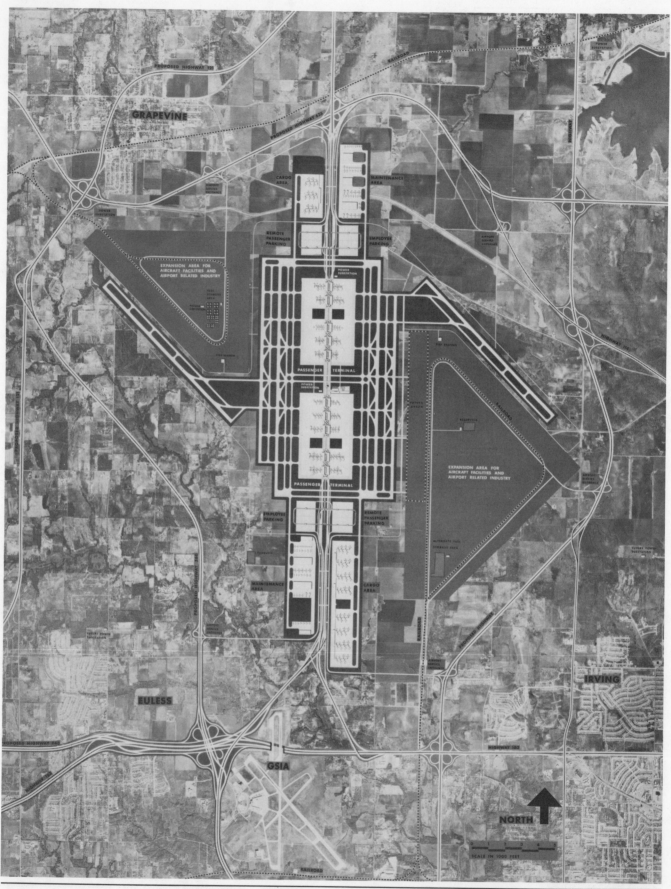

GRAPEVINE

EULESS

GSIA

IRVING

EXPANSION AREA FOR
AIRCRAFT FACILITIES AND
AIRPORT RELATED INDUSTRY

EXPANSION AREA FOR
AIRCRAFT FACILITIES AND
AIRPORT RELATED INDUSTRY

CARGO
AREA

MAINTENANCE
AREA

REMOTE
PASSENGER
PARKING

EMPLOYEE
PARKING

PASSENGER TERMINAL

PASSENGER TERMINAL

EMPLOYEE
PARKING

REMOTE
PASSENGER
PARKING

MAINTENANCE
AREA

CARGO
AREA

NORTH

SCALE IN 1000 FEET

TIPPETTS-ABBOTT-McCARTHY-STRATTON

DANIEL, MANN, JOHNSON, AND MENDENHALL

Schematics

3

After a program has been established with the client to ascertain the requirements of the project, the architect produces the so-called schematic design studies (drawings). The schematics are preliminary, illustrating the scale and relationship of the project's components for approval by all parties involved. Once the schematics are approved, preliminary development documents are produced.

Just like sketches, schematic drawings may be sketchy or very detailed to fix and describe the size and character of the entire project in relation to structural, mechanical, and electrical systems; material; cost; expected income; and so on. They may also consist of various alternate solutions for the same problem.

The main purpose of sketches though is to organize space requirements and develop good relationships between various functions within the building and to the exterior environment. Presently most schematics are executed in colors, by using different colors for the various traffic patterns and/or various activities.

Schematics are very useful and the most important drawings produced during the design process for communication among the various consultants working on the job. Depending on the architect, schematics may vary in quality and quantity for a particular design. The following section shows some samples as well as a complete set produced by architect Fred Lappin for the office of Daniel, Mann, Johnson, and Mendenhall.

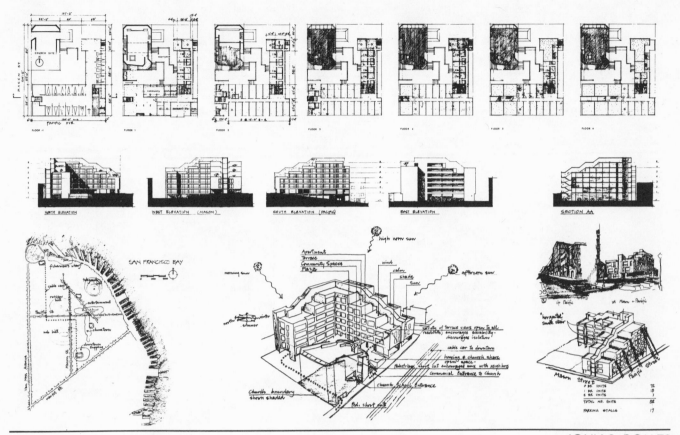

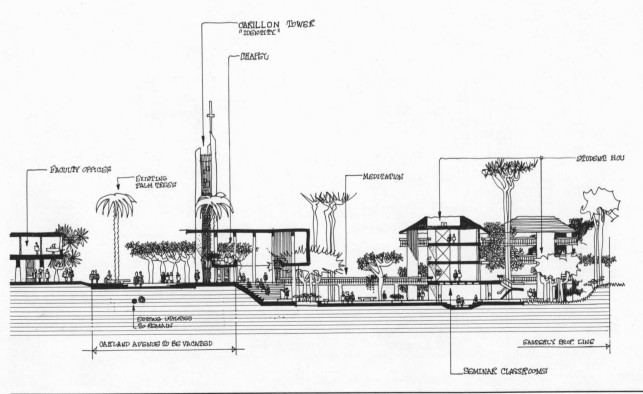

A. QUINCY JONES

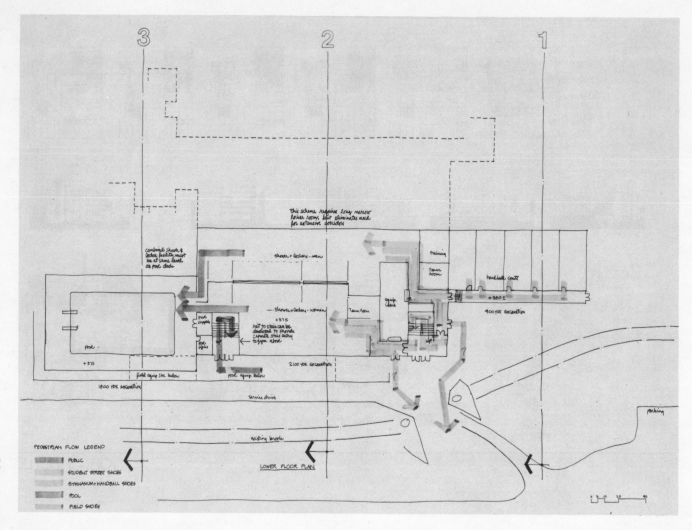

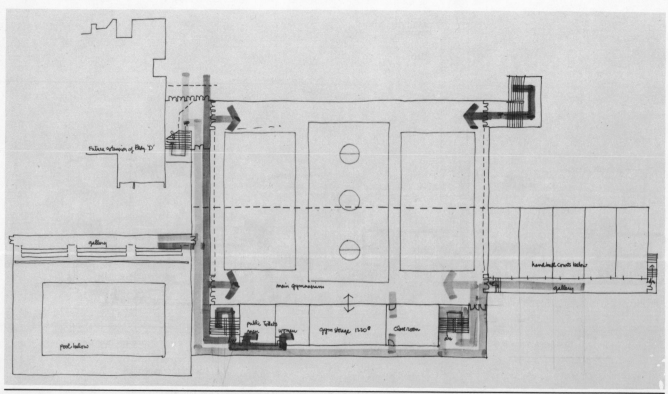

DANIEL, MANN, JOHNSON, AND MENDENHALL

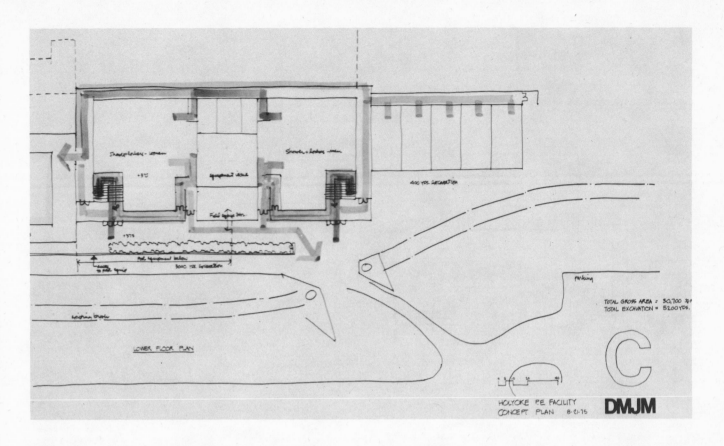

LOWER FLOOR PLAN

Shower + lockers - women   Shower + lockers - men

equipment issue

Field equipment issue

400 YDS. EXCAVATION

+3'0"

+3'0"

Pool equipment below

3000 SF. GYMNASIUM

existing brook

parking

TOTAL GROSS AREA = 30,700 SF
TOTAL EXCAVATION = 5200 YDS.

C

HOLYOKE P.E. FACILITY
CONCEPT PLAN   8-21-75

DMJM

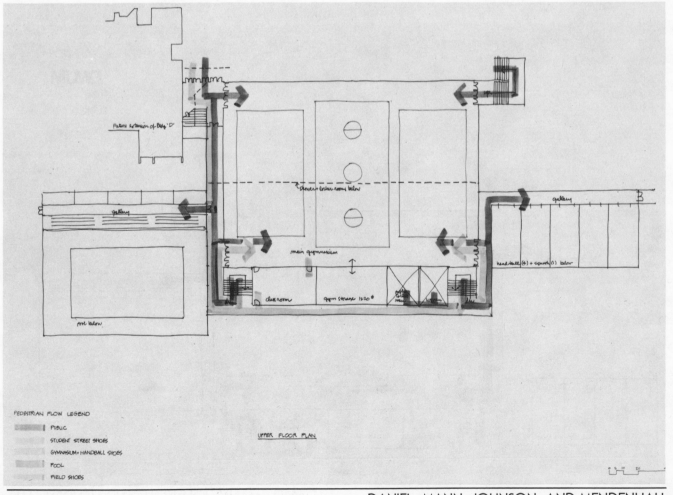

Future extension of Bldg "D"

gallery

Showers + lockers rooms below

main gymnasium

gallery

handball (4) + squash (1) below

pool below

class room

gym storage 1320 SF

UPPER FLOOR PLAN

PEDESTRIAN FLOW LEGEND

PUBLIC

STUDENT STREET SHOES

GYMNASIUM + HANDBALL SHOES

POOL

FIELD SHOES

DANIEL, MANN, JOHNSON, AND MENDENHALL

64

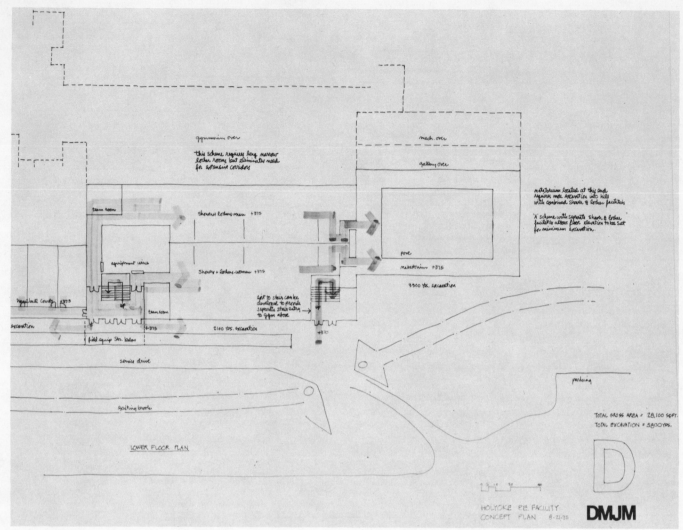

this scheme requires long narrow locker rooms but eliminates need for extensive corridors

team room

Showers & lockers-men +375

equipment room

Showers & lockers-women +375

handball courts +373

team room

excavation

+375

field equip stor below

2100 yds. excavation

service drive

existing brook

LOWER FLOOR PLAN

gymnasium over

mech over

gallery over

natatorium located at this end requires more excavation into hill with combined shower & locker facilities

'A' scheme with separate shower & locker facilities allows floor elevation to be set for minimum excavation.

pool

natatorium +375

3300 yds. excavation

apt to stairs can be developed to provide separate stair entry to gym above

up

+370

parking

TOTAL GROSS AREA = 28,100 SQ.FT.
TOTAL EXCAVATION = 5800 YDS.

D

HOLYOKE P.E. FACILITY
CONCEPT PLAN 8-21-75

DMJM

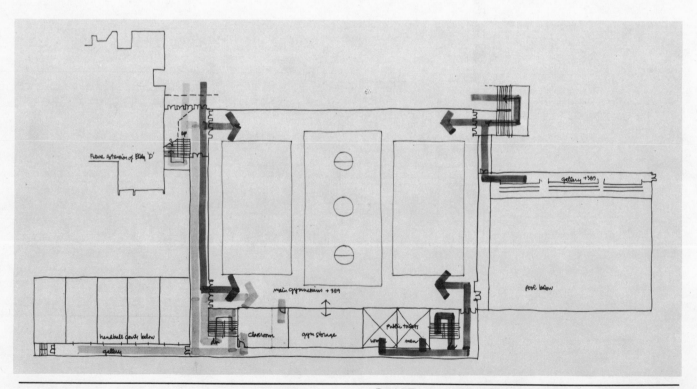

Future extension of Bldg 'D'

gallery +389

main gymnasium +389

handball courts below

gallery

Classroom

gym storage

public toilets

women

men

pool below

DANIEL, MANN, JOHNSON, AND MENDENHALL

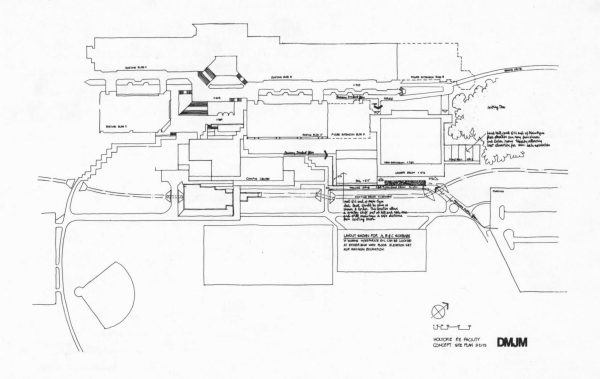

HOLYOKE P.E. FACILITY
CONCEPT SITE PLAN 8-21-75

DMJM

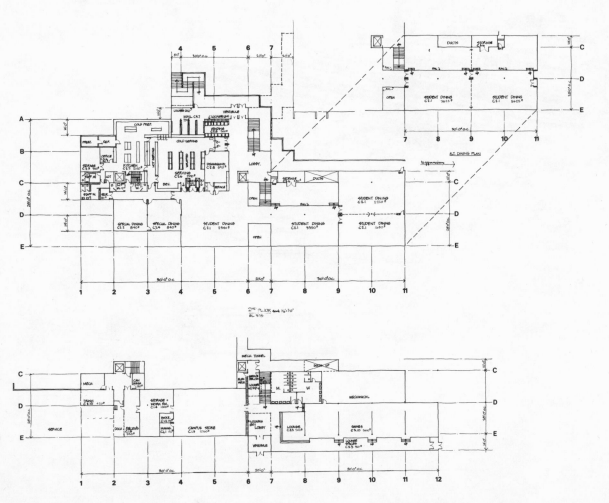

DANIEL, MANN, JOHNSON, AND MENDENHALL

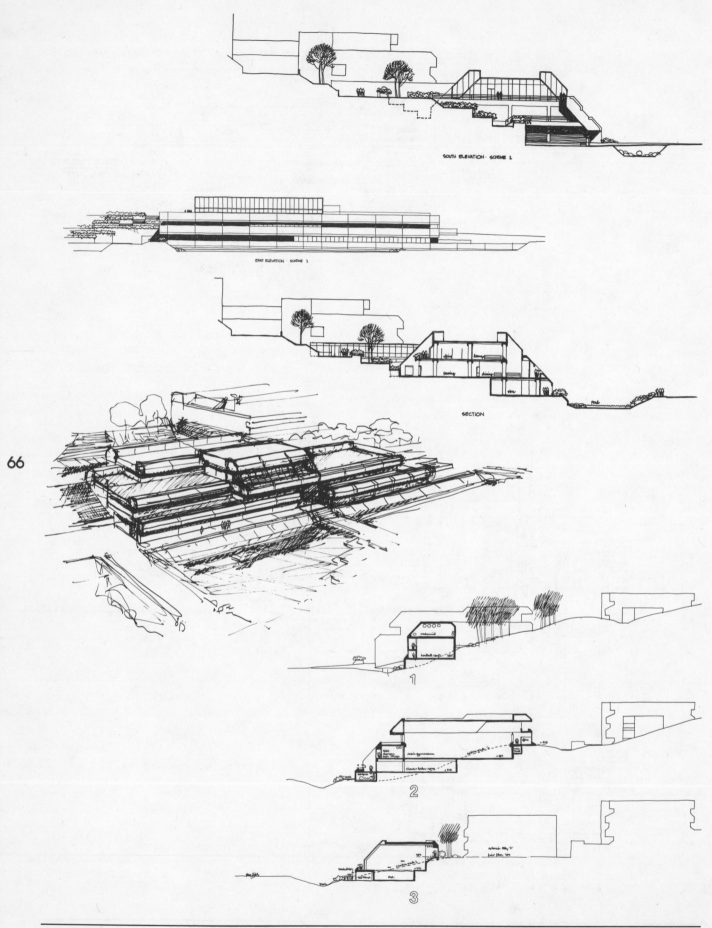

SOUTH ELEVATION · SCHEME 1

EAST ELEVATION · SCHEME 1

SECTION

1

2

3

66

DANIEL, MANN, JOHNSON, AND MENDENHALL

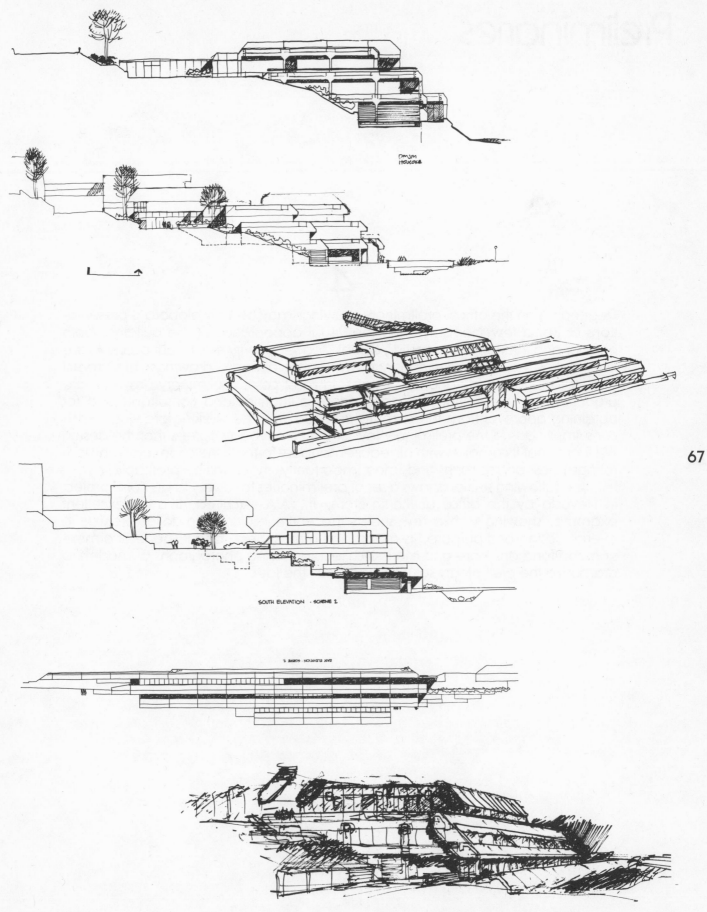

SOUTH ELEVATION · SCHEME 2

67

DANIEL, MANN, JOHNSON, AND MENDENHALL

Preliminaries

4

Depending on the office, preliminary drawings may be very elaborate presentations or just a few sheets showing the visual appearance of the building, both exterior and interior, or suggesting actual "space" activity that might occur. As the title implies, however, preliminary drawings are already "drawings" but are still subject to further study and/or changes. In most cases preliminary drawings are produced for consultation with the various authorities and consultants and for obtaining approval from the client to proceed with the working drawings. Each consultant adds to the preliminary layout until everybody agrees that the design will work; that it complies with all requirements set forth by the code, environmental agencies, and so forth; and, most importantly, that it will be profitable.

The following section shows a set of preliminaries for a very large hotel project in Nevada by the office of Martin Stern, Jr., AIA, Architect. It is an excellent example, showing with a few sheets the entire multimillion-dollar project, its overall design and purpose, its mood and atmosphere, and its general dimension and function. More and more architects are using photographs of models to dramatize the preliminary solution and "sell" the idea.

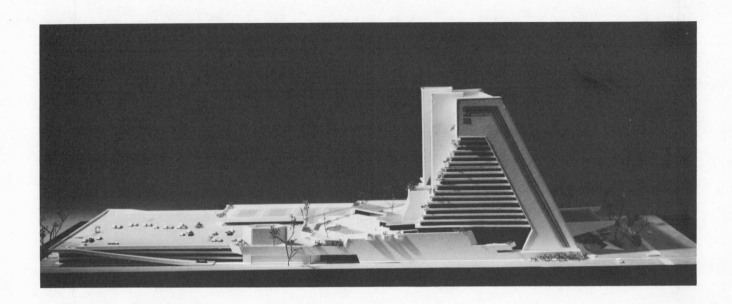

XANADU HOTEL · CASINO
LAS VEGAS, NEVADA

MARTIN STERN JR., A.I.A.
ARCHITECT & ASSOCIATES

sk 1

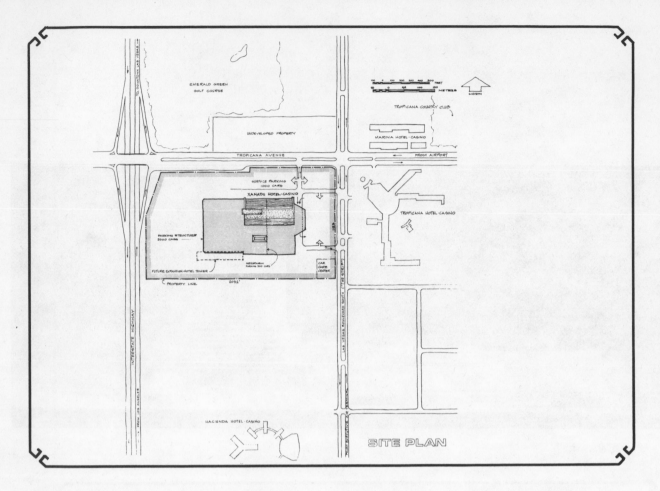

EMERALD GREEN
GOLF COURSE

UNDEVELOPED PROPERTY

TROPICANA COUNTRY CLUB

MARINA HOTEL-CASINO

FROM AIRPORT

TROPICANA AVENUE

SURFACE PARKING
1000 CARS

XANADU HOTEL-CASINO

TROPICANA HOTEL-CASINO

PARKING STRUCTURE
2000 CARS

FUTURE EXPANSION-HOTEL TOWER

SUBTERRANEAN
PARKING 500 CARS

CAR
CARE
CENTER

PROPERTY LINE

HACIENDA HOTEL-CASINO

SITE PLAN

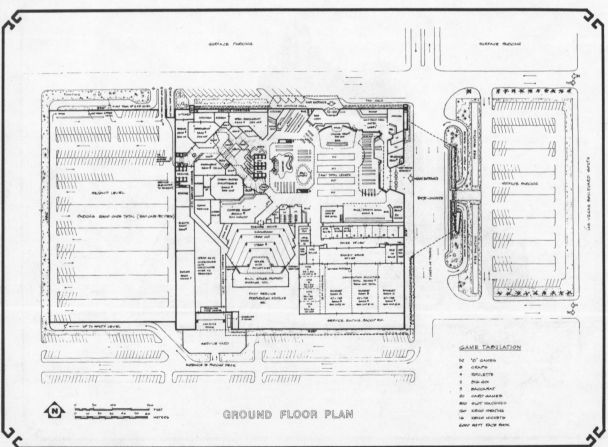

SURFACE PARKING

SURFACE PARKING

GROUND LEVEL

PARKING 5800 CARS TOTAL (500 CARS PER TIER)

SURFACE PARKING

SERVICE YARD

GAME TABULATION

52   "21" GAMES
8   CRAPS
4   ROULETTE
2   BIG SIX
5   BACCARAT
20   CARD GAMES
800   SLOT MACHINES
150   KENO SEATS
16   KENO TICKETS
6000 SQ FT RACE BOOK

GROUND FLOOR PLAN

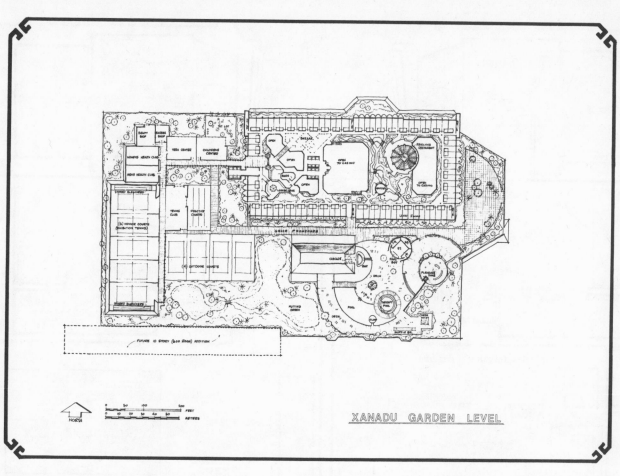

XANADU GARDEN LEVEL

CASINO AND ATRIUM

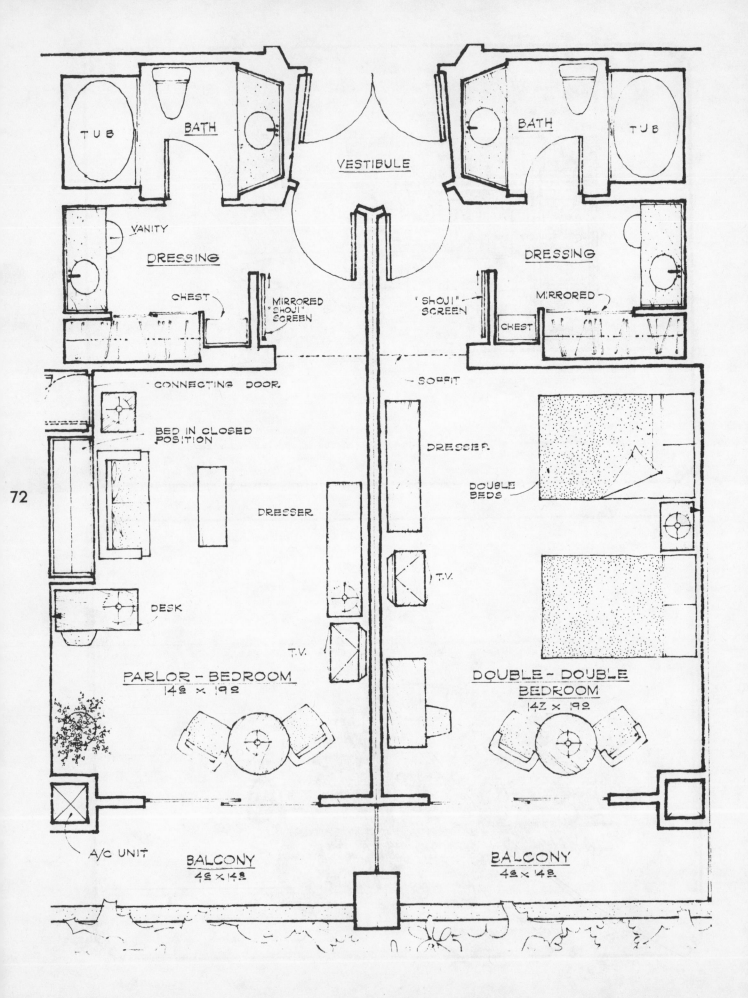

TUB

BATH

VESTIBULE

BATH

TUB

VANITY

DRESSING

CHEST

MIRRORED "SHOJI" SCREEN

DRESSING

"SHOJI" SCREEN

MIRRORED

CHEST

CONNECTING DOOR.

SOFFIT

BED IN CLOSED POSITION

DRESSER

DRESSER

DOUBLE BEDS

DESK

DRESSER

DOUBLE BEDS

T.V.

T.V.

72

PARLOR - BEDROOM
14⁸ × 19⁹

DOUBLE - DOUBLE
BEDROOM
14³ × 19⁹

A/C UNIT

BALCONY
4⁹ × 14⁹

BALCONY
4⁹ × 14⁹

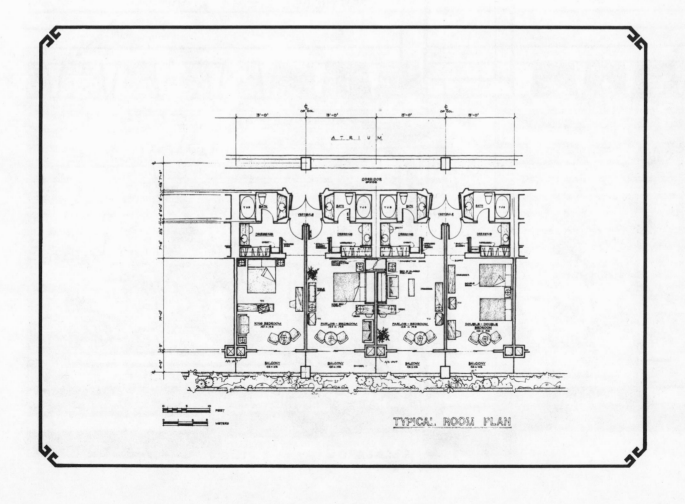

TYPICAL ROOM PLAN

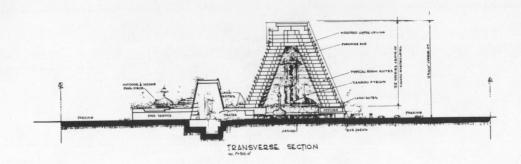

TRANSVERSE SECTION
sc. 1"=50.0'

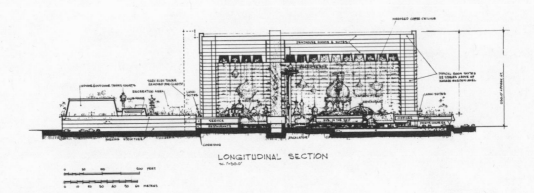

LONGITUDINAL SECTION
sc. 1"=50.0'

74

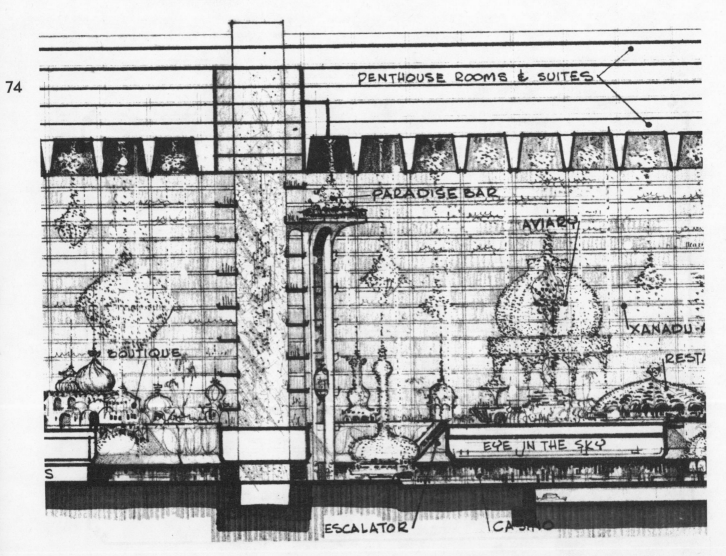

PENTHOUSE ROOMS & SUITES

PARADISE BAR

AVIARY

XANADU A

BOUTIQUE

RESTA

EYE IN THE SKY

S

ESCALATOR   CASINO

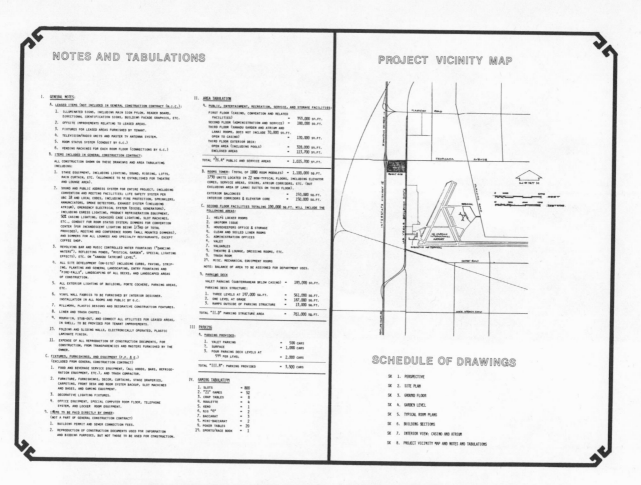

NOTES AND TABULATIONS

I. GENERAL NOTES:

A. LEASED ITEMS (NOT INCLUDED IN GENERAL CONSTRUCTION CONTRACT (N.I.C.)):
1. ILLUMINATED SIGNS, INCLUDING MAIN SIGN PYLON, READER BOARD, DIRECTIONAL IDENTIFICATION SIGNS, BUILDING FACADE GRAPHICS, ETC.
2. OFFSITE IMPROVEMENTS RELATING TO LEASED AREAS.
3. FIXTURES FOR LEASED AREAS FURNISHED BY TENANT.
4. TELEVISION/RADIO UNITS AND MASTER TV ANTENNA SYSTEM.
5. ROOM STATUS SYSTEM (CONDUIT BY G.C.)
6. VENDING MACHINES FOR EACH ROOM FLOOR (CONNECTIONS BY G.C.)

B. ITEMS INCLUDED IN GENERAL CONSTRUCTION CONTRACT:
ALL CONSTRUCTION SHOWN ON THESE DRAWINGS AND AREA TABULATING INCLUDING:
1. STAGE EQUIPMENT, INCLUDING LIGHTING, SOUND, RIGGING, LIFTS, RAIN CURTAIN, ETC. (ALLOWANCE TO BE ESTABLISHED FOR THEATRE AND LOUNGE AREA).
2. SOUND AND PUBLIC ADDRESS SYSTEM FOR ENTIRE PROJECT, INCLUDING CONVENTION AND MEETING FACILITIES; LIFE SAFETY SYSTEM PER UBC 18 AND LOCAL CODES, INCLUDING FIRE PROTECTION, SPRINKLERS, ANNUNCIATORS, SMOKE DETECTORS, EXHAUST SYSTEM (DIESEL GENERATORS), EMERGENCY ELECTRICAL SYSTEM (INCLUDING ATRIUM), INCLUDING EGRESS LIGHTING, PRODUCT REFRIGERATION EQUIPMENT, 50% CASINO LIGHTING, CASHIERS CAGE LIGHTING, SLOT MACHINES, ETC., CONDUIT FOR ROOM STATUS SYSTEM; DIMMERS FOR CONVENTION CENTER (FOR INCANDESCENT LIGHTING BEING 1/3RD OF TOTAL PROVIDED), MEETING AND CONFERENCE ROOMS (WALL MOUNTED DIMMERS), AND DIMMERS FOR ALL LOUNGES AND SPECIALTY RESTAURANTS, EXCEPT COFFEE SHOP.
3. REVOLVING BAR AND MUSIC CONTROLLED WATER FOUNTAINS ("DANCING WATERS"), REFLECTING PONDS, "MYSTICAL GARDEN", SPECIAL LIGHTING EFFECTS), ETC. ON "XANADU (ATRIUM) LEVEL".
4. ALL SITE DEVELOPMENT (ON-SITE) INCLUDING CURBS, PAVING, STRIPING, PLANTING AND GENERAL LANDSCAPING, ENTRY FOUNTAINS AND "FIRE-FALLS", LANDSCAPING OF ALL DECKS, AND LANDSCAPED AREAS OF CONSTRUCTION.
5. ALL EXTERIOR LIGHTING OF BUILDING, PORTE COCHERE, PARKING AREAS, ETC.
6. VINYL WALL FABRICS TO BE FURNISHED BY INTERIOR DESIGNER. INSTALLATION IN ALL ROOMS AND PUBLIC BY G.C.
7. MILLWORK, PLASTIC DESIGNS AND DECORATIVE CONSTRUCTION FEATURES.
8. LINEN AND TRASH CHUTES.
9. ROUGH-IN, STUB-OUT, AND CONNECT ALL UTILITIES FOR LEASED AREAS, IN SHELL, TO BE PROVIDED FOR TENANT IMPROVEMENTS.
10. FOLDING AND SLIDING WALLS, ELECTRONICALLY OPERATED, PLASTIC LAMINATE FINISH.
11. EXPENSE OF ALL REPRODUCTION OF CONSTRUCTION DOCUMENTS, FOR CONSTRUCTION, FROM TRANSPARENCIES AND MASTERS FURNISHED BY THE OWNER.

C. FIXTURES, FURNISHINGS, AND EQUIPMENT (F.F.& E.)
(EXCLUDED FROM GENERAL CONSTRUCTION CONTRACT)
1. FOOD AND BEVERAGE SERVICE EQUIPMENT, (ALL HOODS, BARS, REFRIGERATION EQUIPMENT, ETC.), AND TRASH COMPACTOR.
2. FURNITURE, FURNISHINGS, DECOR, CURTAINS, STAGE DRAPERIES, CARPETING, FRONT DESK AND ROOM SYSTEM BACKUP, SLOT MACHINES AND BASES, AND GAMING EQUIPMENT.
3. DECORATIVE LIGHTING FIXTURES.
4. OFFICE EQUIPMENT, SPECIAL COMPUTER ROOM FLOOR, TELEPHONE SYSTEM, AND LOCKER ROOM EQUIPMENT.

D. ITEMS TO BE PAID DIRECTLY BY OWNER:
(NOT A PART OF GENERAL CONSTRUCTION CONTRACT)
1. BUILDING PERMIT AND SEWER CONNECTION FEES.
2. REPRODUCTION OF CONSTRUCTION DOCUMENTS USED FOR INFORMATION AND BIDDING PURPOSES, BUT NOT THOSE TO BE USED FOR CONSTRUCTION.

II. AREA TABULATION

A. PUBLIC, ENTERTAINMENT, RECREATION, SERVICE, AND STORAGE FACILITIES:

FIRST FLOOR (CASINO, CONVENTION AND RELATED FACILITIES) = 353,000 SQ.FT.
SECOND FLOOR (ADMINISTRATION AND SERVICE) = 100,000 SQ.FT.
THIRD FLOOR (XANADU GARDEN AND ATRIUM AND LANAI ROOMS, DOES NOT INCLUDE 30,000 SQ.FT. OPEN TO CASINO) = 120,000 SQ.FT.
THIRD FLOOR EXTERIOR DECK:
OPEN AREA (INCLUDING POOLS) = 328,000 SQ.FT.
ENCLOSED AREAS = 113,700 SQ.FT.

TOTAL "II.A" PUBLIC AND SERVICE AREAS = 1,015,700 SQ.FT.

B. ROOMS TOWER: (TOTAL OF 1880 ROOM MODULES) = 1,100,000 SQ.FT.
1750 UNITS LOCATED IN 22 NON-TYPICAL FLOORS, INCLUDING ELEVATOR CORES, SERVICE AREAS, STAIRS, ATRIUM CORRIDORS, ETC. (BUT EXCLUDING AREA OF LANAI SUITES ON THIRD FLOOR).
EXTERIOR BALCONIES = 150,000 SQ.FT.
INTERIOR CORRIDORS & ELEVATOR CORE = 150,000 SQ.FT.

C. SECOND FLOOR FACILITIES TOTALING 100,000 SQ.FT. WILL INCLUDE THE FOLLOWING AREAS:
1. HELPS LOCKER ROOMS
2. UNIFORM ISSUE
3. HOUSEKEEPERS OFFICE & STORAGE
4. CLEAN AND SOILED LINEN ROOMS
5. ADMINISTRATION OFFICES
6. VALET
7. VALUABLES
8. THEATRE & LOUNGE, DRESSING ROOMS, ETC.
9. TRASH ROOM
10. MISC. MECHANICAL EQUIPMENT ROOMS
NOTE: BALANCE OF AREA TO BE ASSIGNED FOR DEPARTMENT USES.

D. PARKING DECK
VALET PARKING (SUBTERRANEAN BELOW CASINO) = 100,000 SQ.FT.
PARKING DECK STRUCTURE:
1. THREE LEVELS AT 187,000 SQ.FT. = 561,000 SQ.FT.
2. ONE LEVEL AT GRADE = 187,000 SQ.FT.
3. RAMPS OUTSIDE OF PARKING STRUCTURE = 13,000 SQ.FT.

TOTAL "II.D" PARKING STRUCTURE AREA = 761,000 SQ.FT.

III. PARKING

A. PARKING PROVIDED:
1. VALET PARKING = 500 CARS
2. SURFACE = 1,000 CARS
3. FOUR PARKING DECK LEVELS AT 575 PER LEVEL = 2,000 CARS

TOTAL "III.A" PARKING PROVIDED = 3,500 CARS

IV. GAMING TABULATION
1. SLOTS = 800
2. "21" GAMES = 52
3. CRAP TABLES = 8
4. ROULETTE = 4
5. KENO = 1
6. BIG "6" = 2
7. BACCARAT = 3
8. MINI-BACCARAT = 2
9. POKER TABLES = 20
10. SPORTS/RACE BOOK = 1

PROJECT VICINITY MAP

SCHEDULE OF DRAWINGS

SK 1. PERSPECTIVE
SK 2. SITE PLAN
SK 3. GROUND FLOOR
SK 4. GARDEN LEVEL
SK 5. TYPICAL ROOM PLANS
SK 6. BUILDING SECTIONS
SK 7. INTERIOR VIEW: CASINO AND ATRIUM
SK 8. PROJECT VICINITY MAP AND NOTES AND TABULATIONS

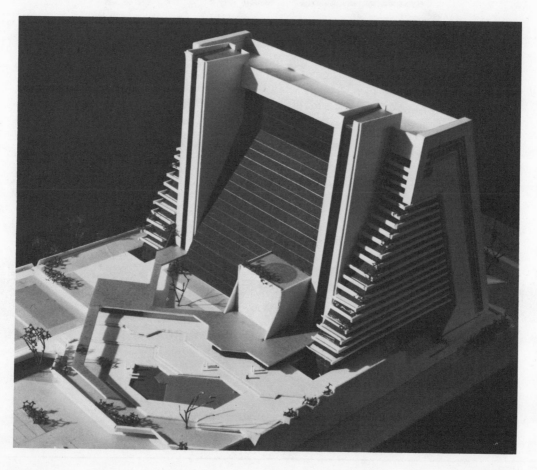

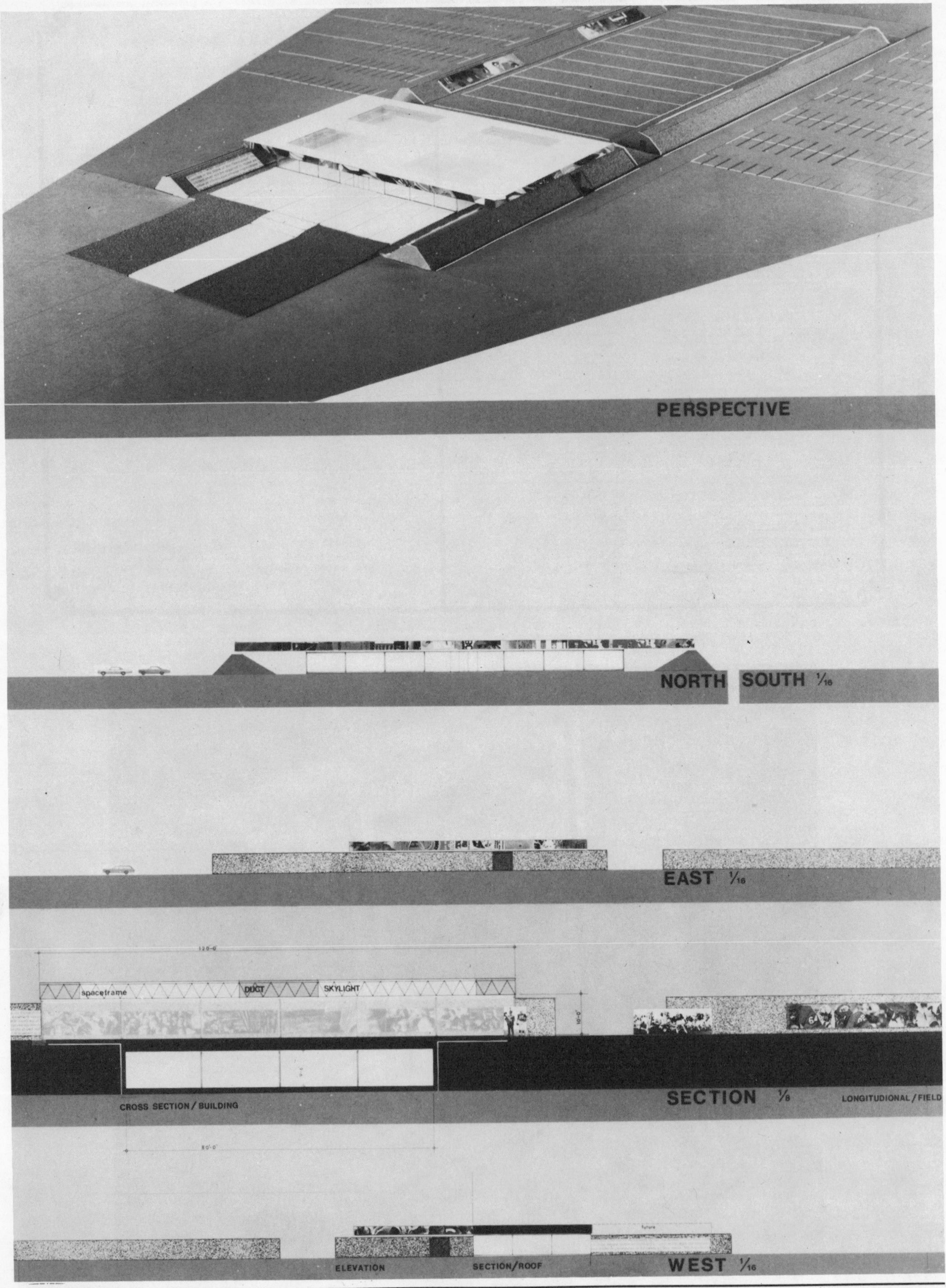

PERSPECTIVE

NORTH SOUTH 1/16

EAST 1/16

spaceframe   DUCT   SKYLIGHT

CROSS SECTION / BUILDING

SECTION 1/8   LONGITUDIONAL / FIELD

ELEVATION   SECTION/ROOF   WEST 1/16

A. M. KEMPER

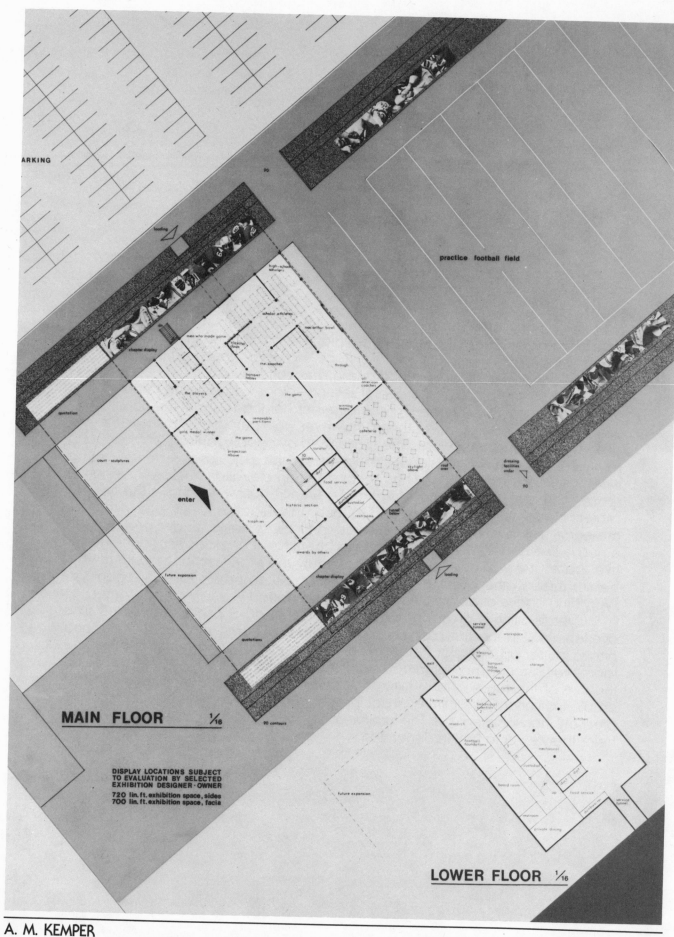

MAIN FLOOR 1/16

DISPLAY LOCATIONS SUBJECT
TO EVALUATION BY SELECTED
EXHIBITION DESIGNER · OWNER

720 lin. ft. exhibition space, sides
700 lin. ft. exhibition space, facia

LOWER FLOOR 1/16

A. M. KEMPER

Floor Plans

5

The word **plan** comes partly from the Latin word **planum**, meaning "level ground" and partly from the French word **planter**, "to plant, fix in place." A "plan" is a drawing fixed on a plane or flat surface. However, the word **plan** is not an accurate description of the actual drawing. The correct word should be **plansection**, because the plan is a horizontal section (plane). In working drawings the plansection is cut through the walls at different heights to show the construction system. In architectural presentation, however, the purpose is to show the enclosed space or, in other words, the space used by people, animals, objects, and so on. For the sake of discussion we could refer to this space as positive space. The walls, columns, and so forth, when cut at a certain elevation, expose a negative space, namely, the very space that in the working drawings shows the type of material used, reinforcing, post, and so forth. This negative space in architectural presentation is always **poché**, mostly a deep black, but at times also profiled with a heavy line between the positive space (the interior or exterior) and the negative space (the wall thickness, etc.). Preferably the plan (section) should always be cut through the building at a height that encompasses all wall openings. Everything above or below this height is shown dotted in one way or another.

Overdetailing is a common mistake in architectural presentation, and so is overlabeling. In the first case nonessential floor patterns, dimension lines, and arrows clutter up the space (room), and in the latter, bad lettering stifles the room. For instance most bathrooms are easily recognized by everybody; seeing the size of the room or one fixture identifies the room and its purpose. In fact simple indications of furniture or equipment in a room can identify its use more precisely than labeling can. The furniture also gives scale to the space and visually helps the viewer to feel its dimension.

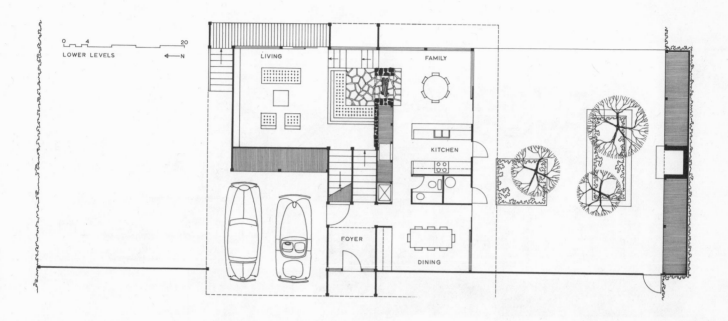

LOWER LEVELS

0 4   20

← N

LIVING

FAMILY

KITCHEN

FOYER

DINING

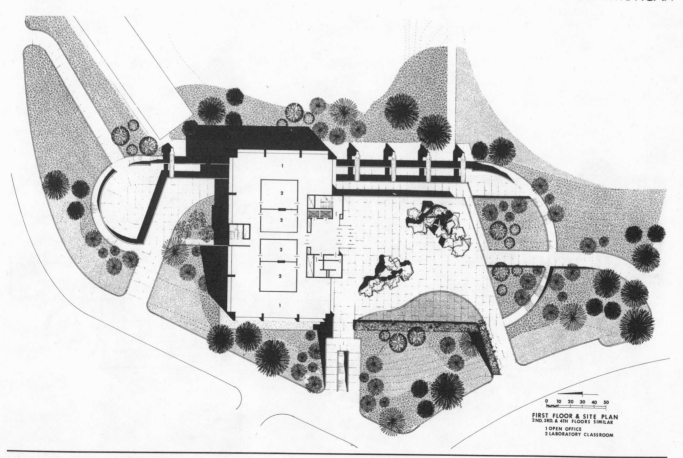

0 10 20 30 40 50

FIRST FLOOR & SITE PLAN
2ND, 3RD, & 4TH FLOORS SIMILAR
1 OPEN OFFICE
2 LABORATORY CLASSROOM

MILTON T. PFLUEGER

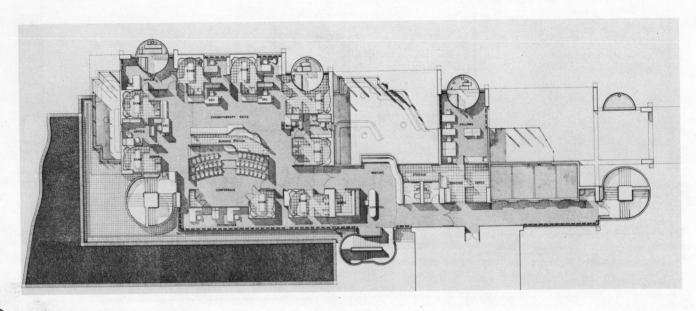

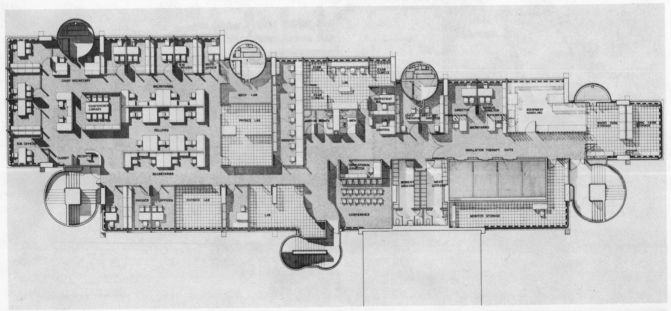

PERRY, DEAN, AND STEWART

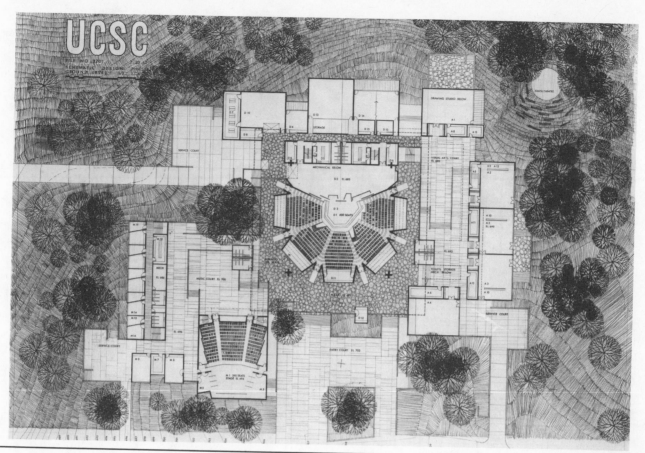

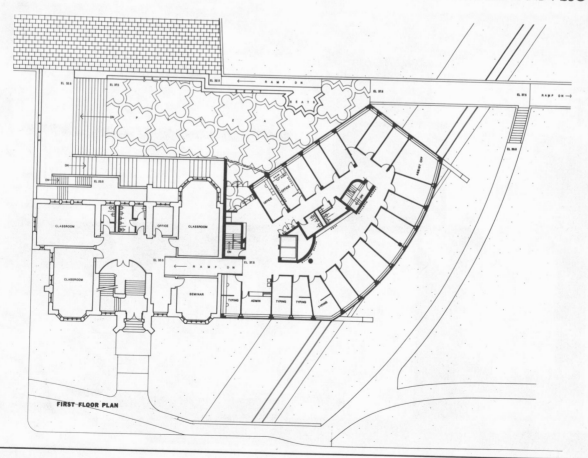

FIRST FLOOR PLAN

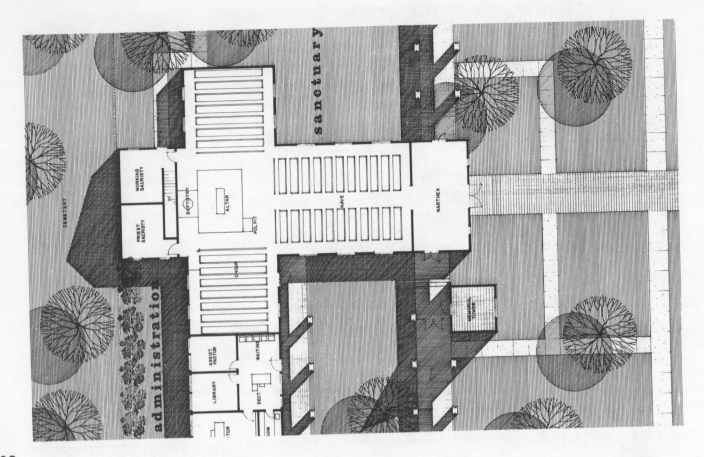

82

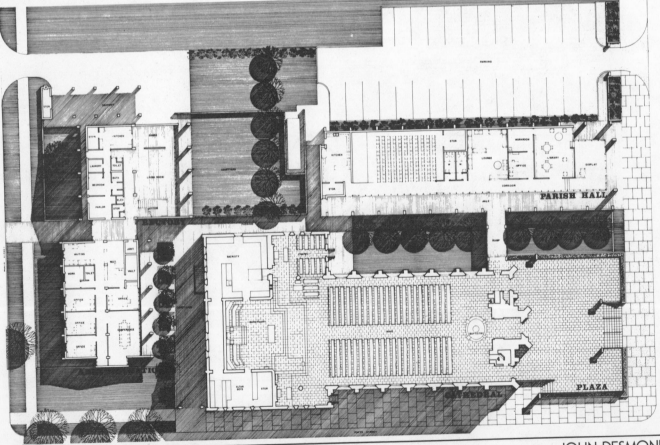

JOHN DESMOND

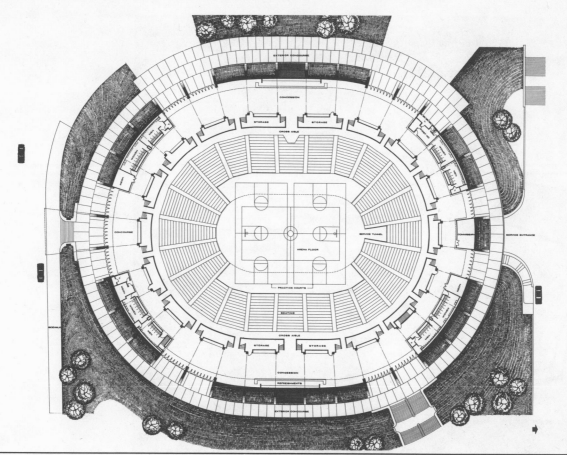

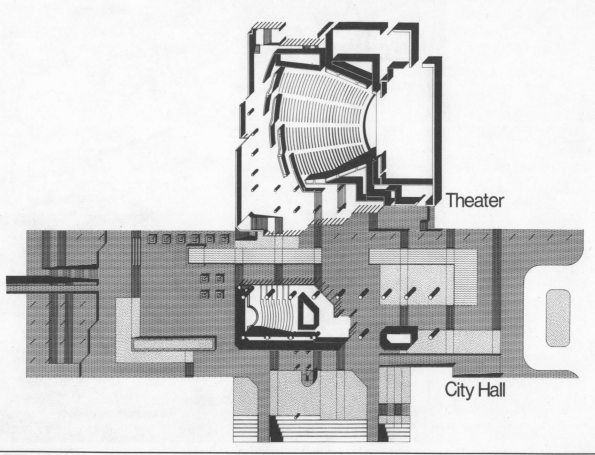

Theater

City Hall

JOHN CASBARIAN   GRUEN ASSOCIATES

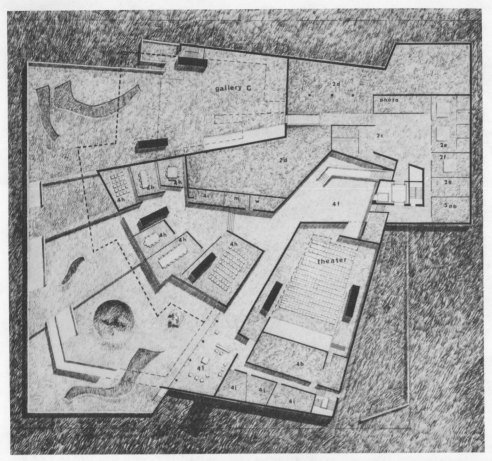

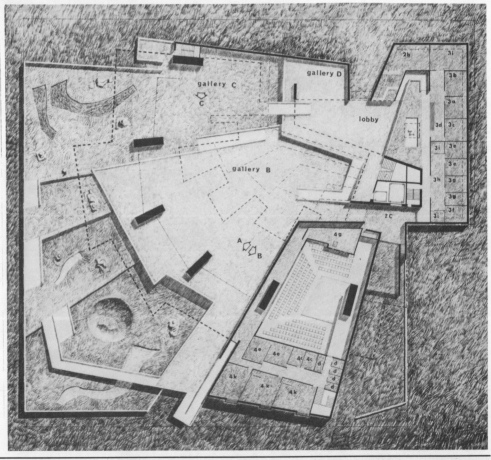

R. L. JORASH AND R. E. WAGNER

MARIO CIAMPI AND ASSOCIATES

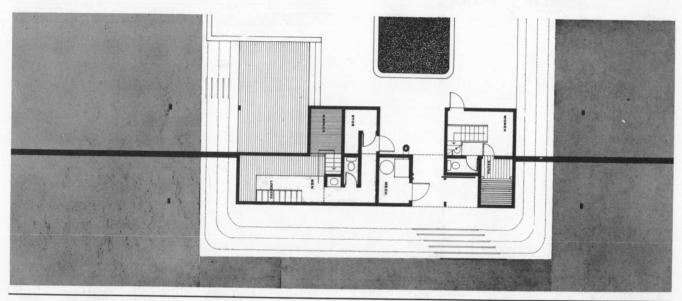

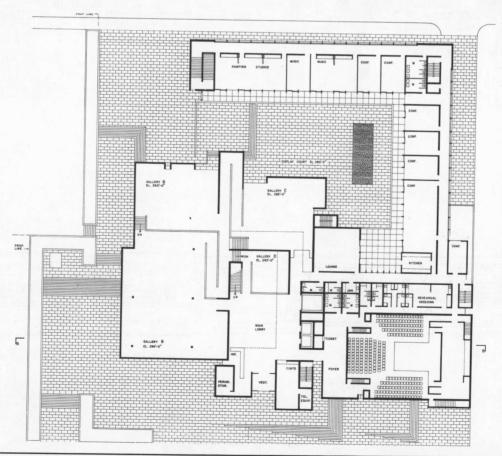

MARVIN HATAMI AND ASSOCIATES

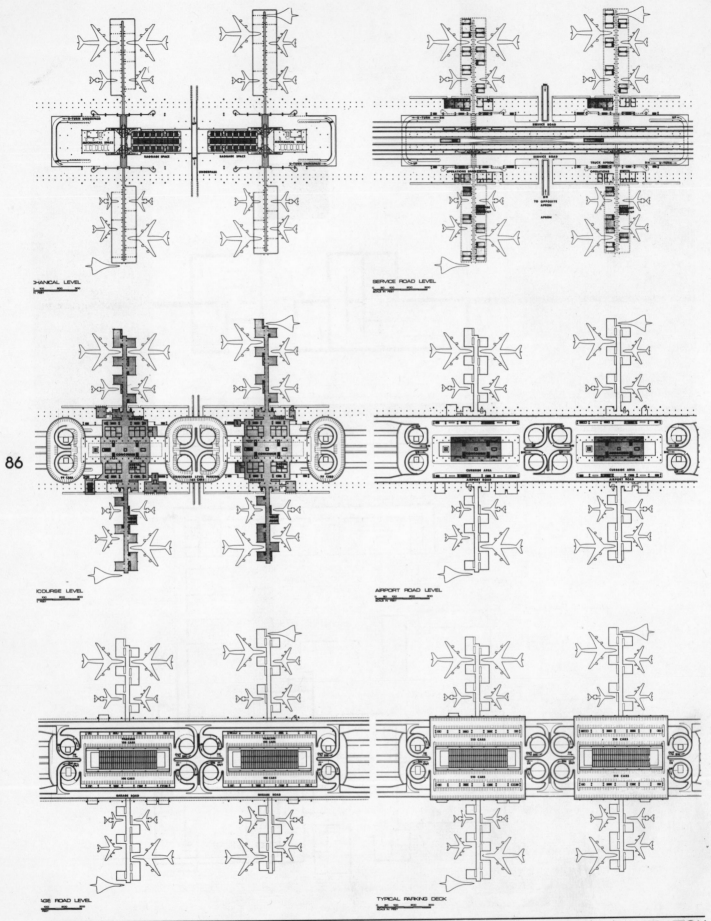

86

MECHANICAL LEVEL

SERVICE ROAD LEVEL

CONCOURSE LEVEL

AIRPORT ROAD LEVEL

GARAGE ROAD LEVEL

TYPICAL PARKING DECK

TIPPETS-ABBETT-McCARTHY-STRATTON

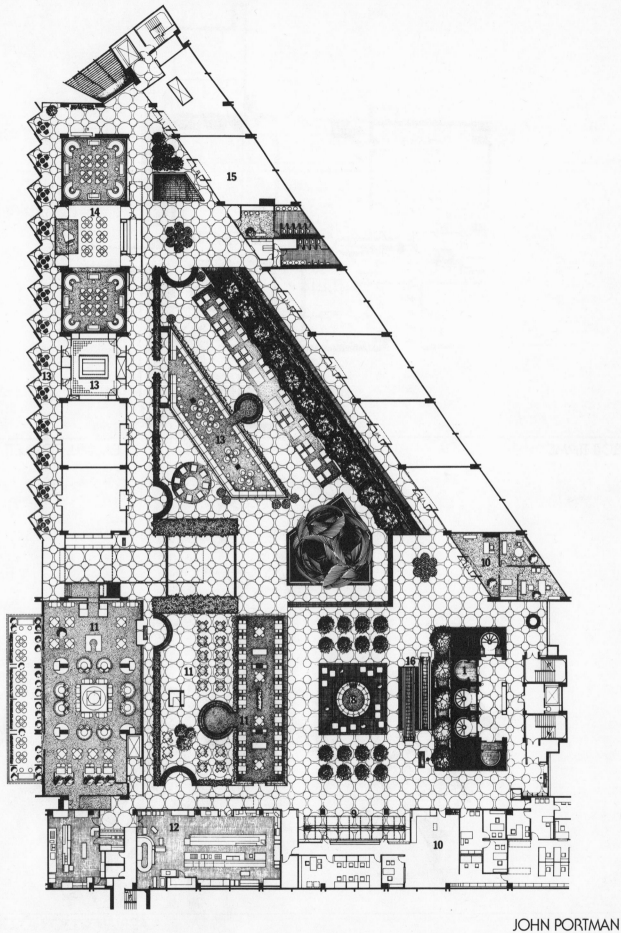

87

JOHN PORTMAN

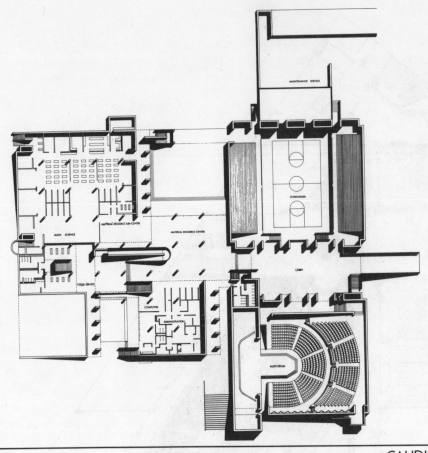

CAUDILL ROWLETT SCOTT

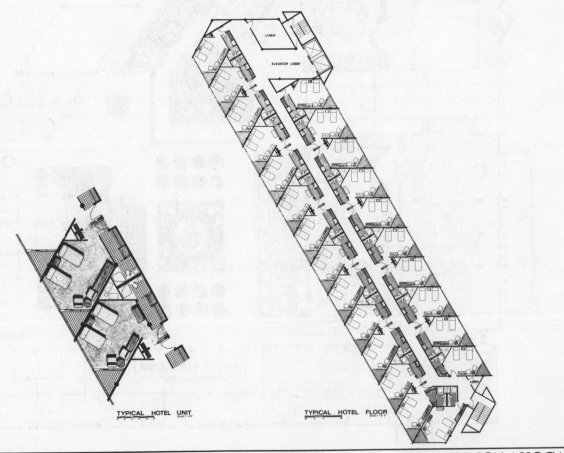

TYPICAL HOTEL UNIT

TYPICAL HOTEL FLOOR

ADRIAN WILSON ASSOCIATES

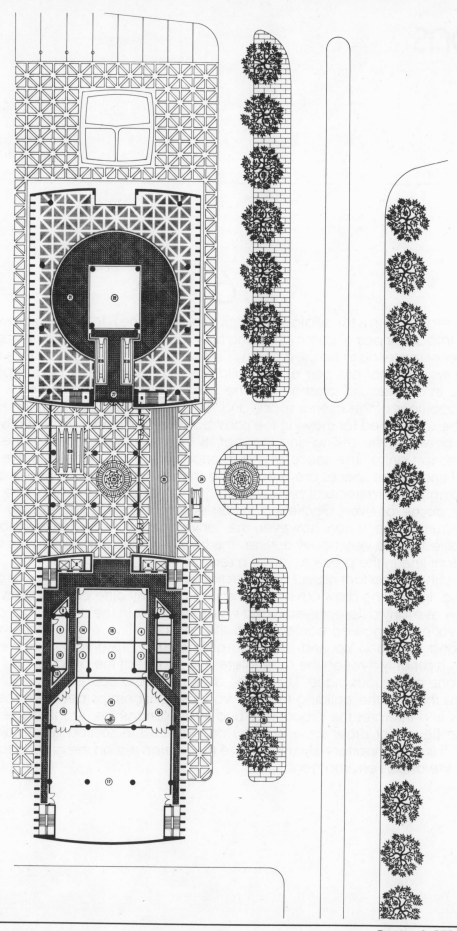

DMJM & PERENTJAN DJAJA

Sections

6

In architectural terms the section is a vertical plan (plane). In working drawings it is a very important part of communicating how the building is to be built. It shows all the interior materials to be used and is filled with instructions and key references to all the systems that are part of the building, such as mechanical and plumbing spaces. In architectural presentation the prime function of the section is to show the proportions of the interior space and, secondarily, the interior finishes. Therefore, the space used for showing the construction system, such as the walls and the space between the ceiling and the roof, is the negative space (for the sake of presentation only). The space of the interior and of the exterior is the positive space, since these spaces are used by the inhabitants of the proposed building. Accordingly, in architectural presentation, just as for plans, the negative space is usually **poché** or even blackened in, at least in the sketching stages. In good architectural presentation, however, the "envelope" of this negative space should be profiled with a very heavy outline. This heavy outline in the section is the most important line in the presentation of a section.

Another important aspect of the section is where the section is cut through the building. In working drawings it is cut through as many different places as possible to show as many different details and systems as exist in the sketch. Thus one may have various staggered portions, and the sectional line might conceivably jog back and forth and up and down. In architectural presentation, however, the section is cut only through the most interesting spaces of the building and preferably in one continuous plane. During the design stage a designer must take many sections through the building to study various relationships between the interior spaces and interpret the proportions and interrelationships. At this stage too, the human figure (or other scale objects) drawn into the section give scale to the space. It is also important always to have the section rest on the ground to relate it to the site and its environment.

90

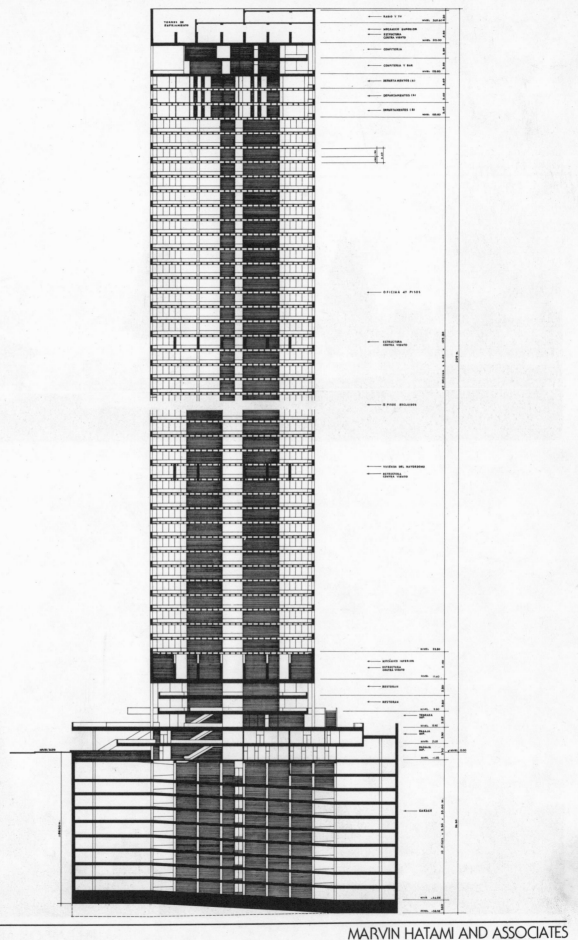

91

MARVIN HATAMI AND ASSOCIATES

RALPH RAPSON AND ASSOCIATES

DANIEL DWORSKY AND ASSOCIATES   93

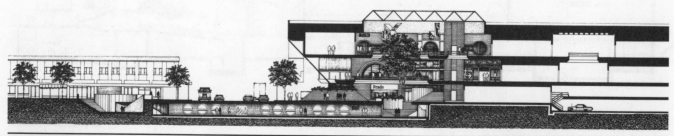

A. JASKIEWICZ   CHARLES KOBER ASSOCIATES

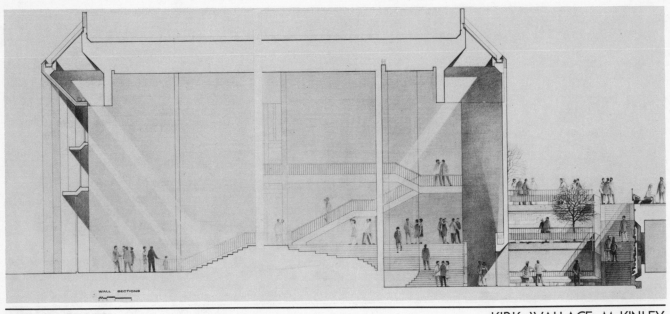

94   MICHAEL DAHER

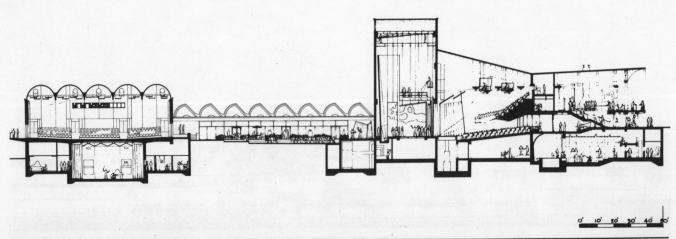

HARRISON AND ABRAMOVITZ

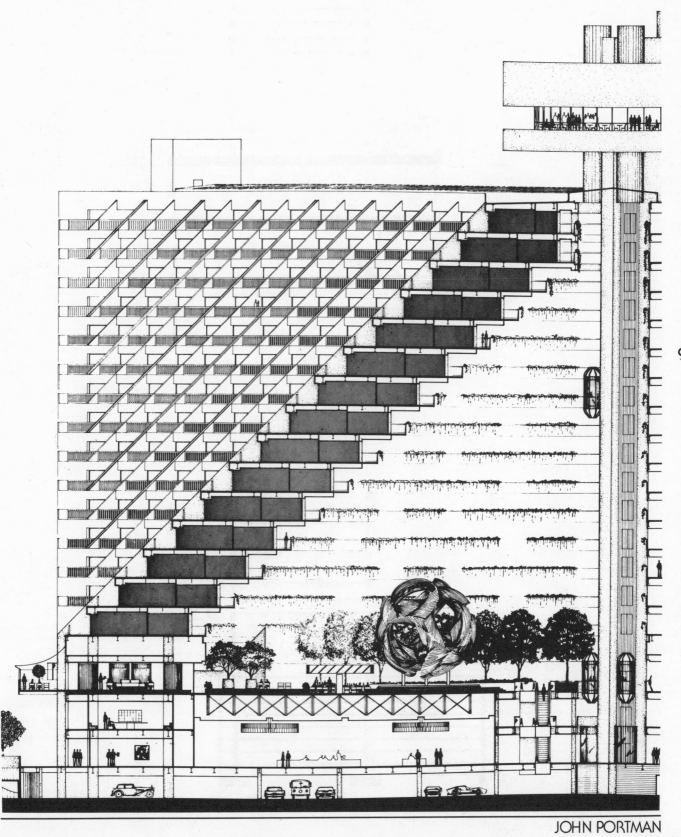

95

JOHN PORTMAN

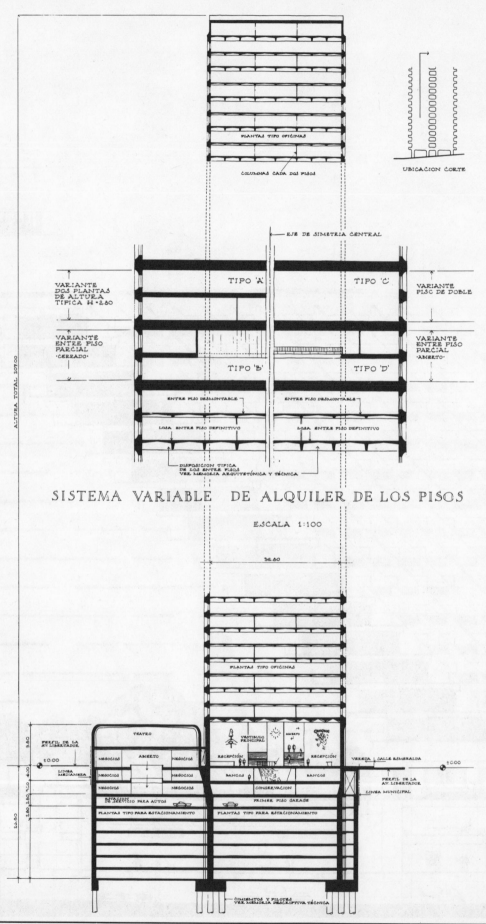

SISTEMA VARIABLE DE ALQUILER DE LOS PISOS

ESCALA 1:100

A. M. KEMPER

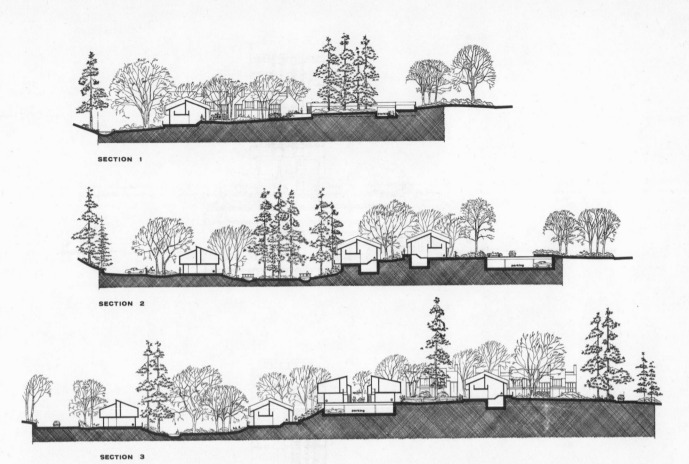

SECTION 1

SECTION 2

SECTION 3

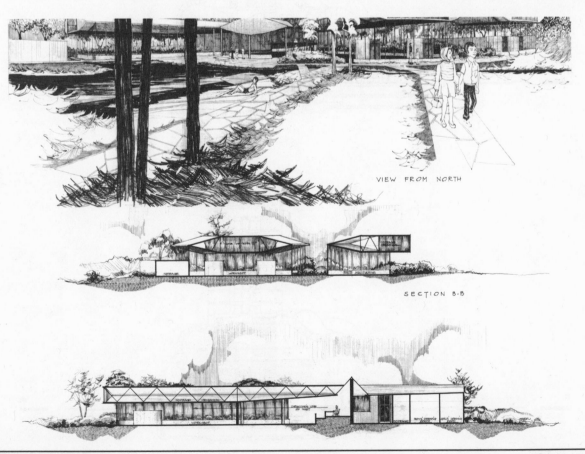

VIEW FROM NORTH

SECTION B-B

ANGELA ZAR

JOHN LAUTNER

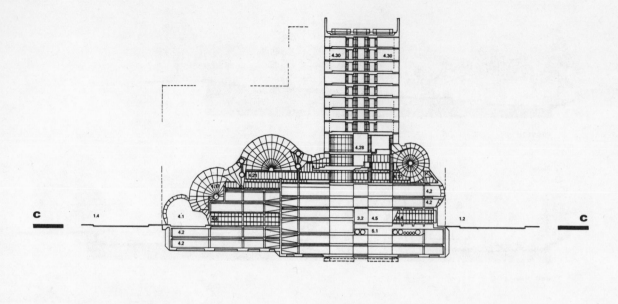

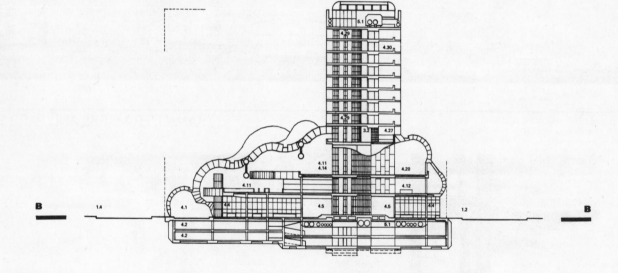

98

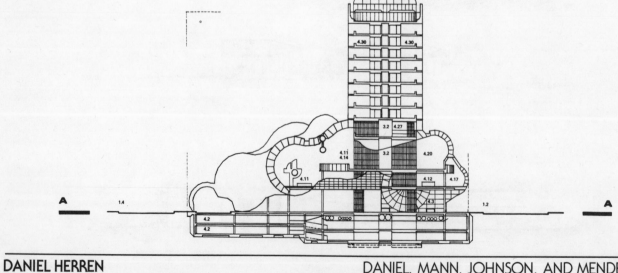

DANIEL HERREN

DANIEL, MANN, JOHNSON, AND MENDENHALL

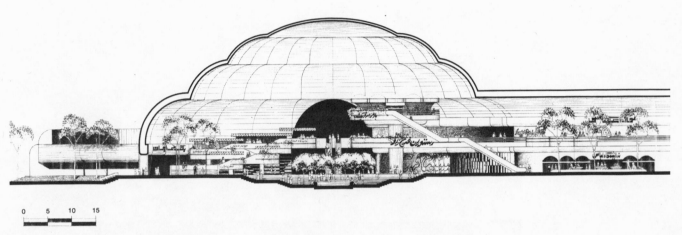

0 5 10 15

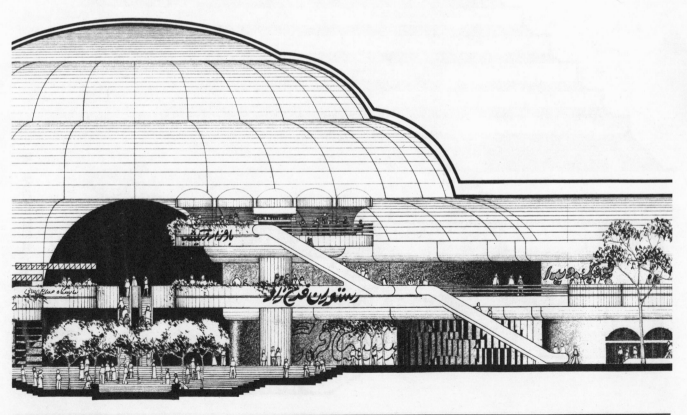

ARIELDA PASTIER

ARCHISYSTEM

100

ARIELDA PASTIER AND JOHN H. SPOHRER

ARCHISYSTEM

ARIELDA PASTIER AND JOHN H. SPOHRER

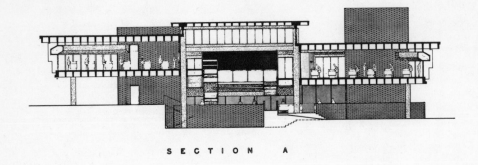

SECTION A

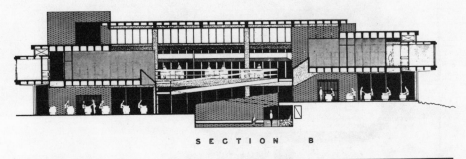

SECTION B

102 MEL FORD   CARL MASTON

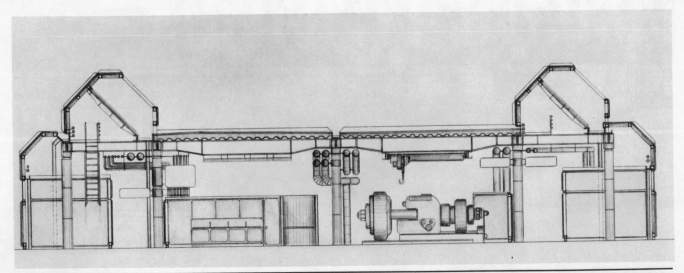

DANIEL HERREN   DANIEL, MANN, JOHNSON, AND MENDENHALL

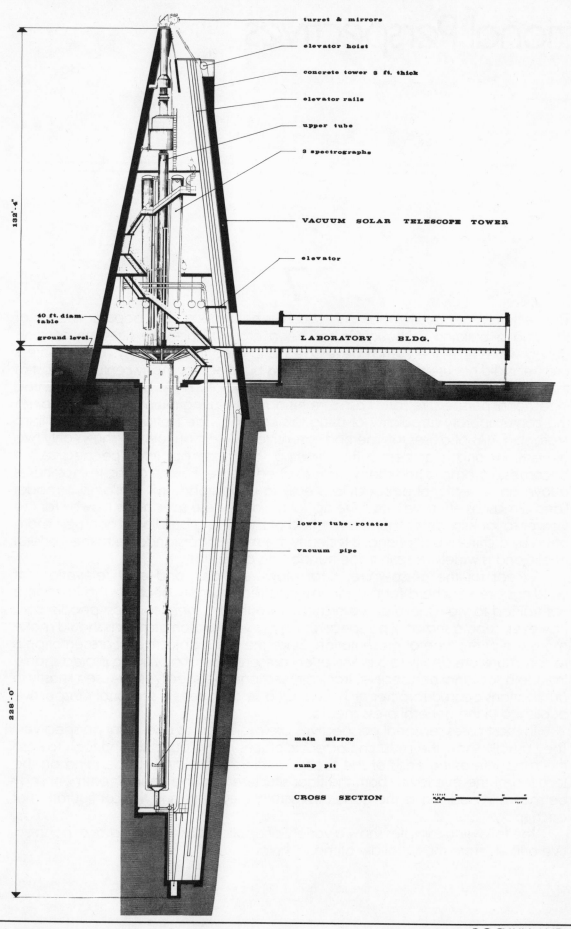

turret & mirrors

elevator hoist

concrete tower 3 ft. thick

elevator rails

upper tube

3 spectrographs

VACUUM SOLAR TELESCOPE TOWER

elevator

40 ft. diam. table

ground level

LABORATORY BLDG.

132'-4"

228'-0"

lower tube - rotates

vacuum pipe

main mirror

sump pit

CROSS SECTION

103

Sectional Perspectives

7

The sectional perspective has only recently become a very popular means of showing a building, although it has been around since the fifteenth century, during which time the French developed and used it extensively. Unfortunately architects did not use this method of showing buildings for many centuries. Most of the work of the contemporary architect Paul Rudolph, FAIA, has been presented in sectional perspective, and I am sure his activity in using this method has inspired the contemporary popularity of using this drawing. The Florida architect William Morgan, FAIA, also uses this method extensively. A section, per se, shows only two dimensions and is at best a flat drawing, but once put into "perspective," it becomes a dramatic and many-dimensioned picture. For the client, in most cases a layman, a sectional perspective is easy to understand. It is similar to a model (and almost as effective), as if the actual building were specially cut away for the viewer to look inside it. That this method of showing a building is not used more often by architects is surprising. It is clearly the most understandable to the general public and is widely used in trade handbooks of all kinds.

Except for the perspective, floor plans, sections, and even elevations of buildings are very hard for most laymen to read, simply because the layman is not trained to view them as we architects would like them to. Most people can, however, read a sectional perspective. For this very reason architects should make more use of this type of presentation. Since the main objective of presentation is to communicate clearly to a client, every presentation of a building project should include a sectional perspective. Ironically sectional perspectives are used mostly in publications geared to other architects. One seldom sees a sectional perspective published in the general press media.

In most cases sectional perspectives are projected as one-point perspectives. They usually show the most characteristic places in the building and look toward the most interesting ends of the spaces within the building. Depending on the location of the eye level, both the floor structure and the ceiling treatment may be shown in addition to the general structural elements and the configuration of each space.

The following samples show a variety of applications of the sectional perspective and illustrate the simplicity of the technique.

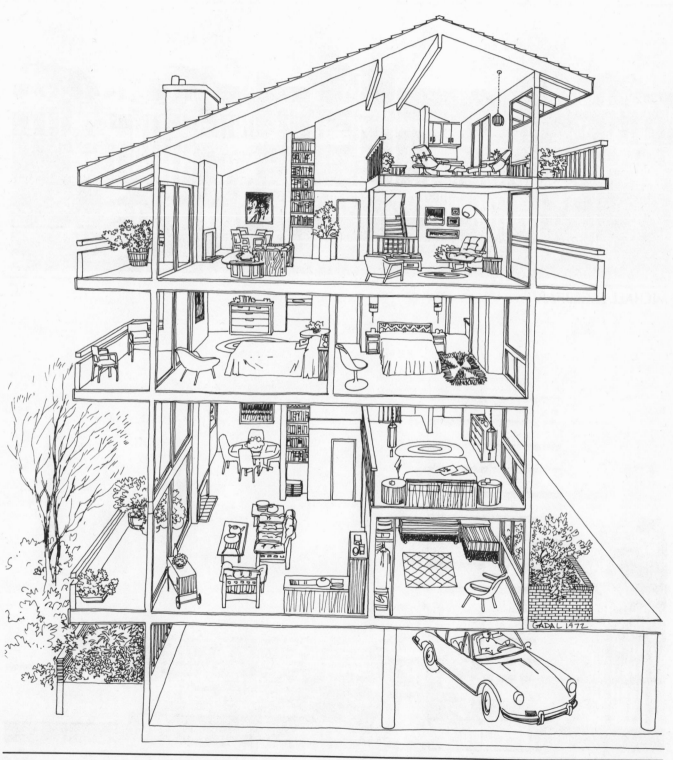

GADAL 1972

CLARK-HEDRIC INC.

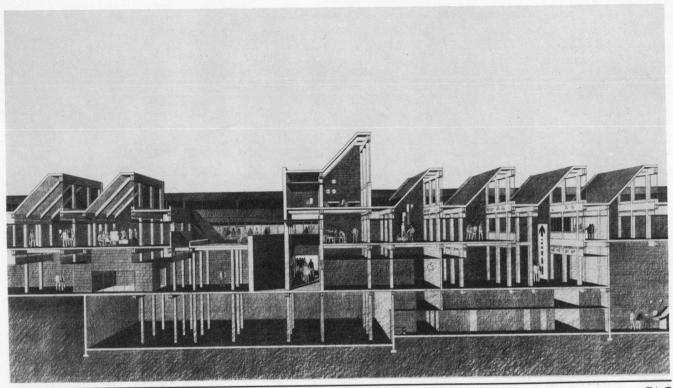

106 MICHAEL F. GEBHART

TAC

T. N. LARSON AND J. SHEEHY

TAC

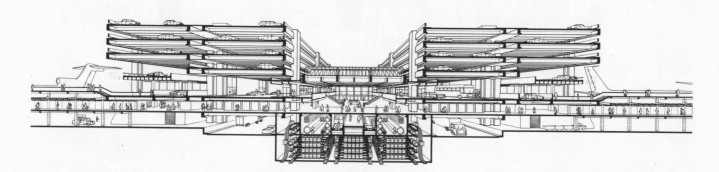

DONALD A. REED

EARL R. FLANSBURGH AND ASSOCIATES

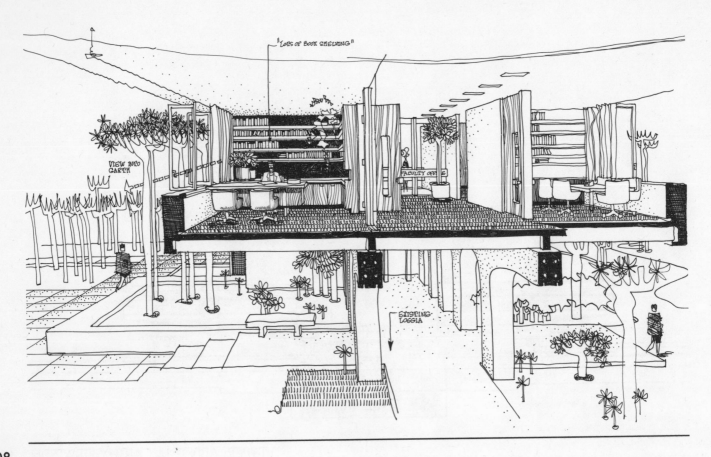

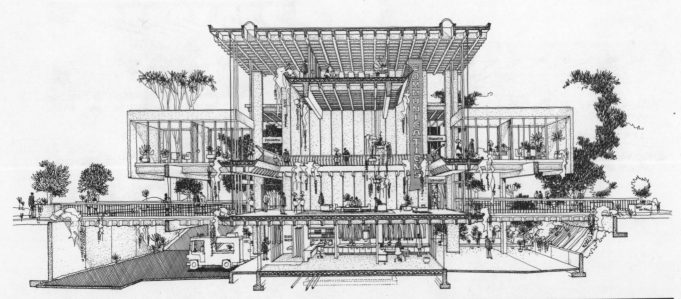

A. QUINCY JONES AND ASSOCIATES

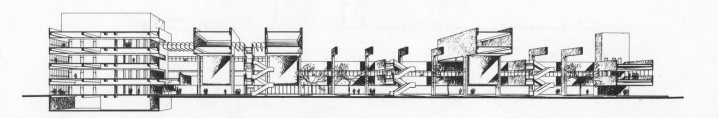

WILLIAM MORGAN

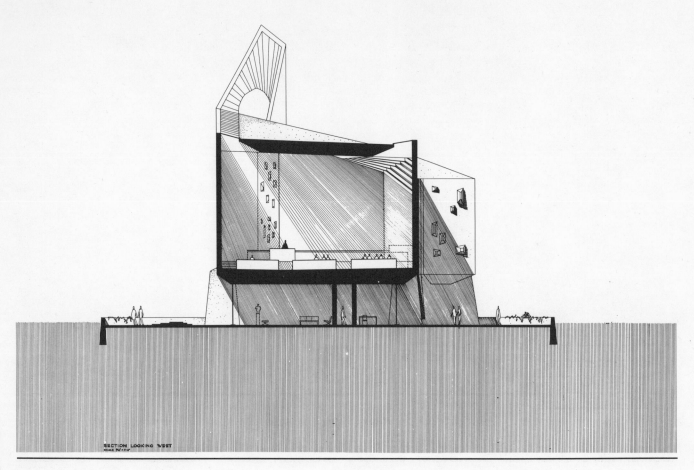

SECTION LOOKING WEST

110

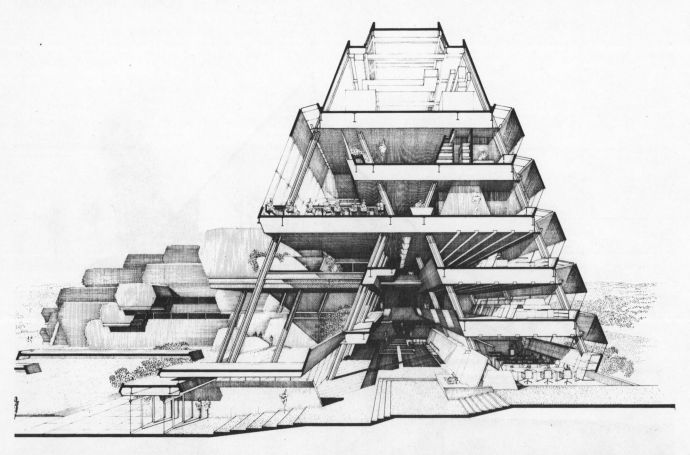

PAUL RUDOLPH

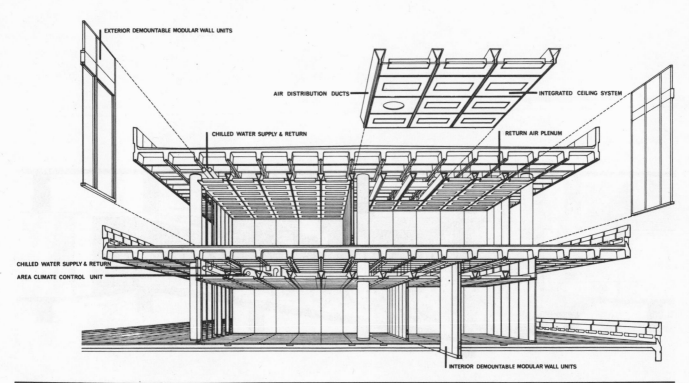

EXTERIOR DEMOUNTABLE MODULAR WALL UNITS

AIR DISTRIBUTION DUCTS

INTEGRATED CEILING SYSTEM

CHILLED WATER SUPPLY & RETURN

RETURN AIR PLENUM

CHILLED WATER SUPPLY & RETURN

AREA CLIMATE CONTROL UNIT

INTERIOR DEMOUNTABLE MODULAR WALL UNITS

DANIEL, MANN, JOHNSON, AND MENDENHALL   111

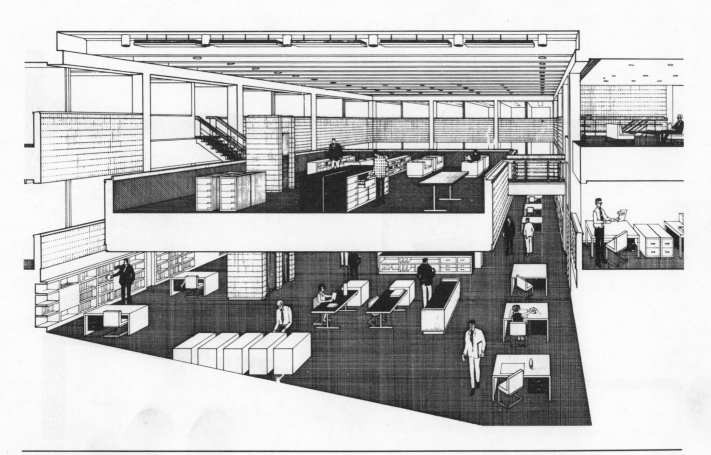

ROBERT C. STEINMETZ   S.M.S.

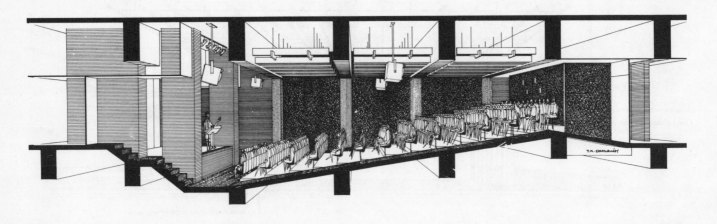

112

T. K. DAHLQUIST

JOHN HASSAN CROWTHER

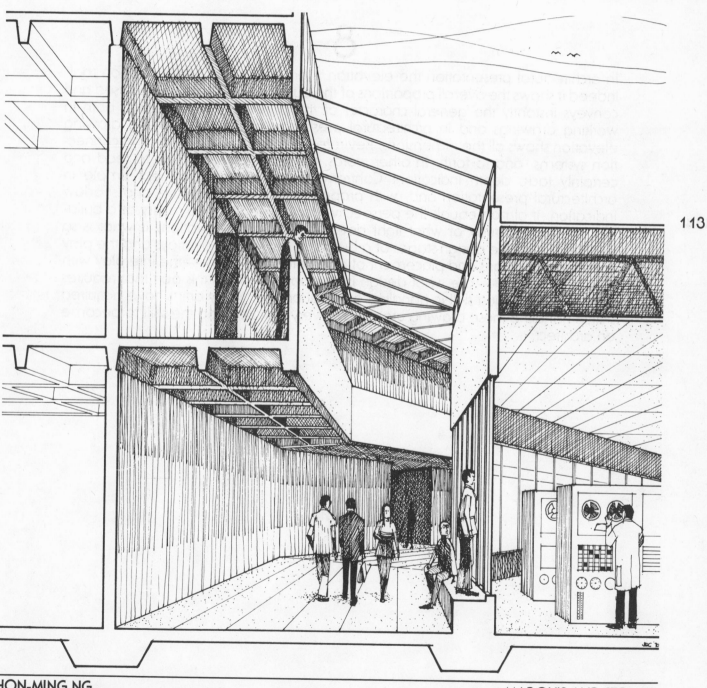

HON-MING NG

MARQUIS AND STOLLER

Elevations

8

In architectural presentation the elevation is an important communication tool. Indeed it shows the overall proportions of the building and the materials used and conveys instantly the general character of the building. This holds true both in working drawings and in architectural presentation. But the working drawing elevation shows all the dimensions, key reference to various details, and connection systems, and so forth. In other words it is very busy and hard to read and certainly lacks depth indication. Contrariwise the elevation is kept simple in architectural presentation and, with proper line value and shade and shadow indication, it almost equals the perspective for delineating the reality of a building. In fact the study of what light does on the form (elevation) is what is so exciting during the design stages of a building. The various overlays and the play with the proportions and placement of open areas (spaces) — the interplay with plan and section — are what design is all about, and it is this part that requires intellect and not just skill in handling a pencil or pen. Many artists have acquired skill in handling these drawing utensils, but very few develop the skill to become an architect.

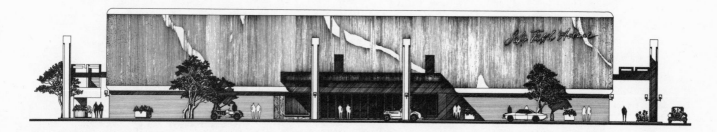

A. JASKIEWICG

CHARLES KOBER ASSOCIATES 115

GRUEN ASSOCIATES

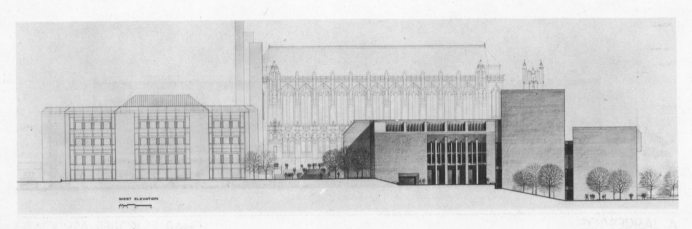

WEST ELEVATION

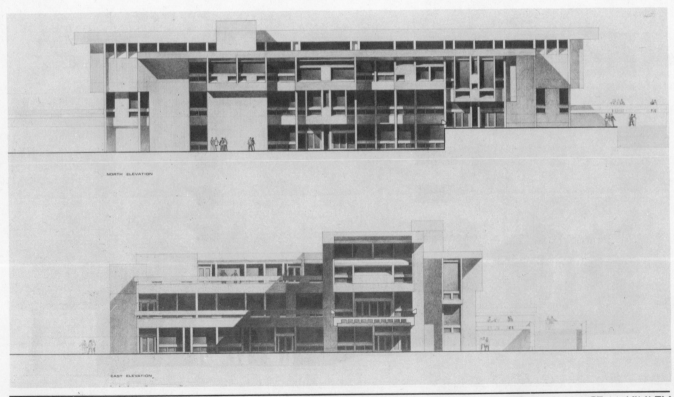

NORTH ELEVATION

EAST ELEVATION

M. D. MAHLER   KIRK-WALLACE-McKINLEY

PERRY, DEAN AND STEWART **117**

RALPH RAPSON AND ASSOCIATES

118

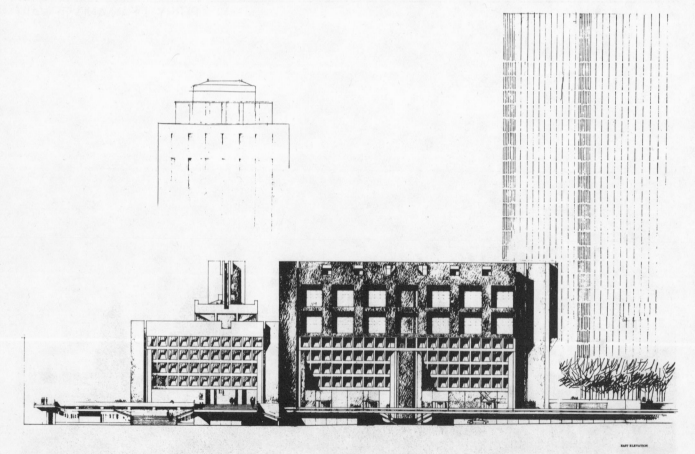

EAST ELEVATION

MITCHELL/GIURGOLA ASSOCIATES

119

120

ADRIAN WILSON ASSOCIATES

121

ADRIAN WILSON ASSOCIATES

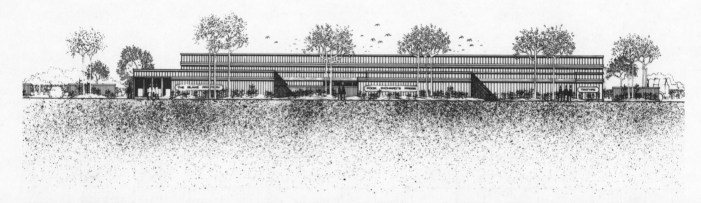

122 BOB KITAMURA

PRIEST, RICHMOND, WOLF AND ROSSI

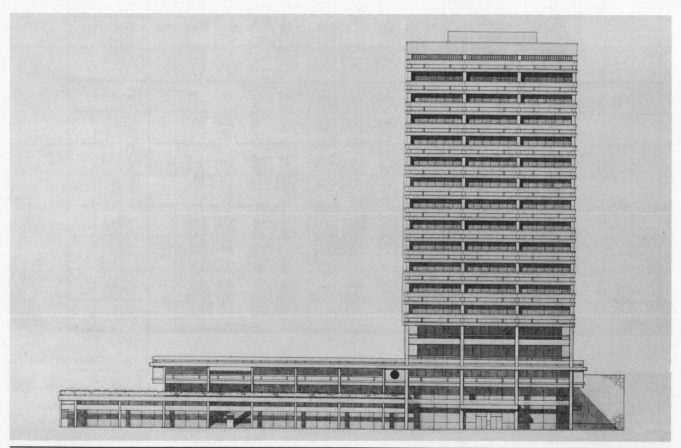

KUNIO MIYOSHI AND DAVE MORIOKA

KAJIMA ASSOCIATES

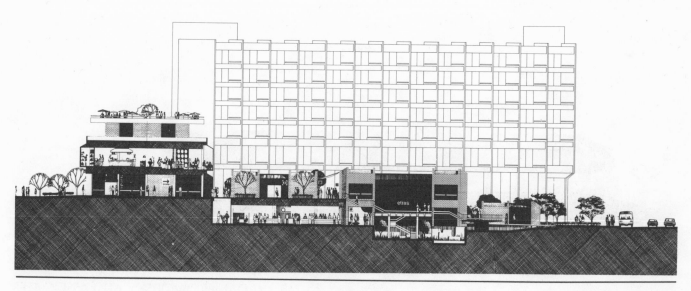

ADRIAN WILSON ASSOCIATES

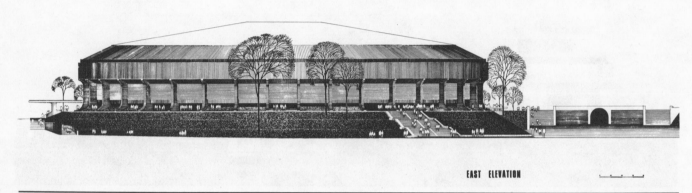

EAST ELEVATION

124

DANIEL DWORSKY AND ASSOCIATES

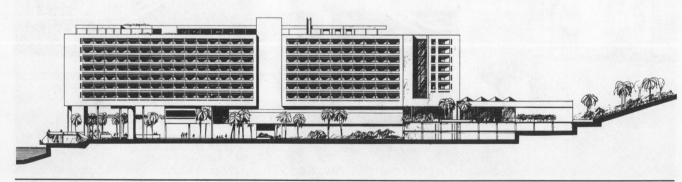

G. DOWNES

TAC

125

KAMNITZER, MARKS, VREELAND, AND LAPPIN

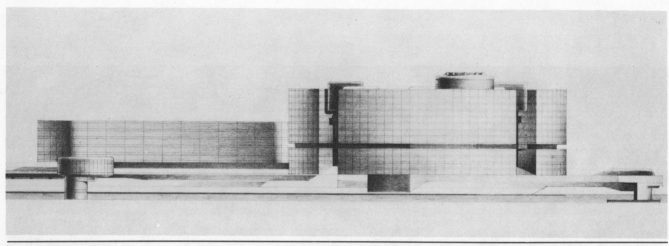

126 P. J. JACOBSON   DANIEL, MANN, JOHNSON, AND MENDENHALL

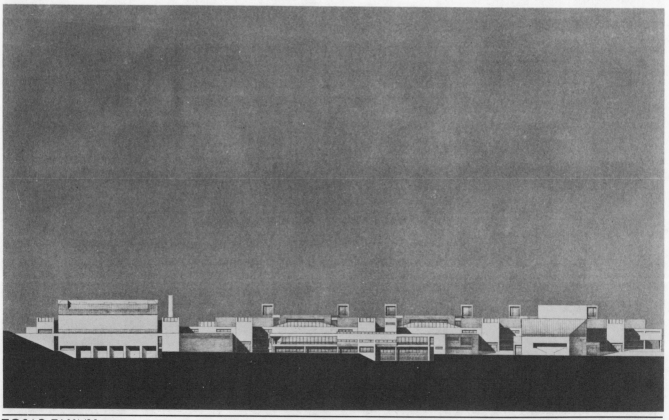

ZOSAR FAHMY   PERRY, DEAN AND STEWART

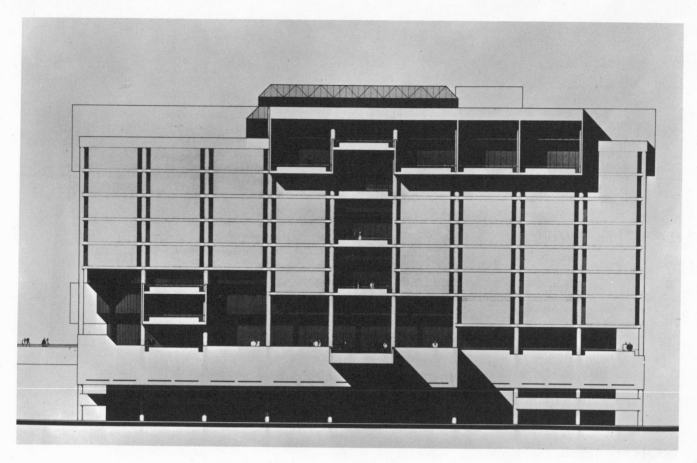

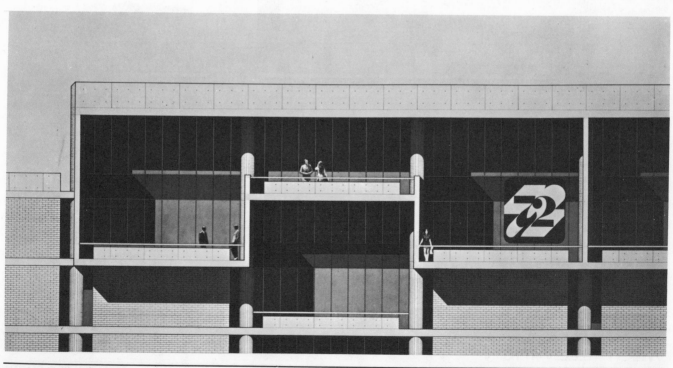

ROBERT KAMINSKY

WELTON BECKET AND ASSOCIATES

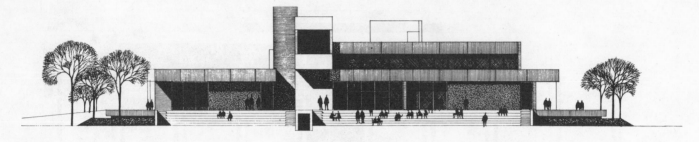

EAST ELEVATION

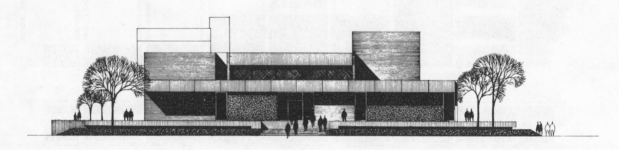

NORTH ELEVATION

128

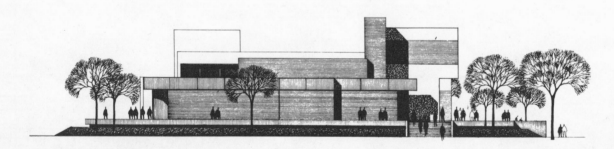

SOUTH ELEVATION

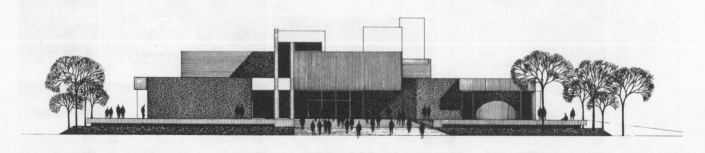

WEST ELEVATION

CHARLES LUCKMAN ASSOCIATES

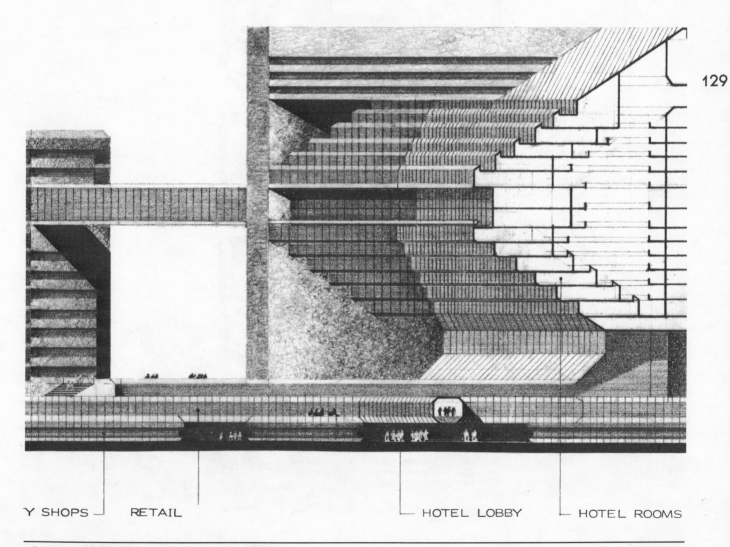

FOURTH STREET   BALBOA THEATER   RETAIL   SHOPS   HORTON SQUARE   HOTEL ROOMS   DEPARTMENT STORE   OFFICE BUILDING   FIRST STREET   CENTRAL FEDERAL

Y SHOPS   RETAIL   HOTEL LOBBY   HOTEL ROOMS

JOHN H. SPOHRER AND DAN CLINGIER   ARCHISYSTEMS

DENIS HARTLEY

ARCHISYSTEMS

DENIS HARTLEY

ARCHISYSTEMS

132

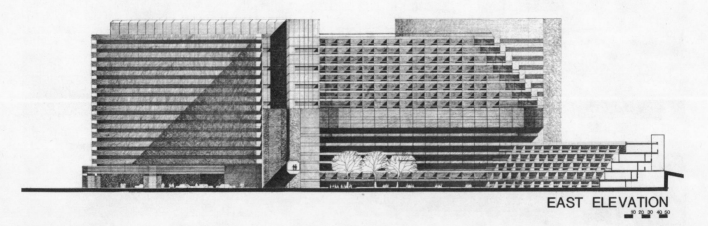

SOUTH ELEVATION

EAST ELEVATION

10 20 30 40 50

JOHN H. SPOHRER

ARCHISYSTEMS

JOHN H. SPOHRER

ARCHISYSTEMS

134

GERALD HORN

CRAIG ELLWOOD ASSOCIATES

NORTH

GERD ERNST   DANIEL, MANN, JOHNSON, AND MENDENHALL

136

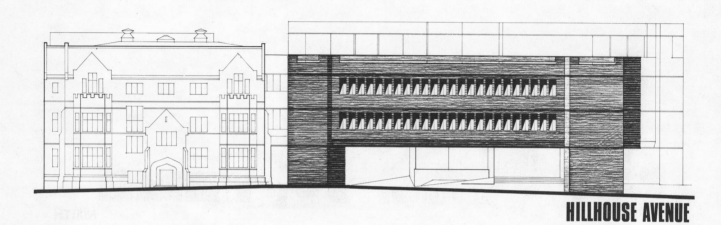

HILLHOUSE AVENUE

BECTON PLAZA

EXISTING

OPEN

LEET OLIVER MEMORIAL HALL

HILLHOUSE AVENUE

ALLEY ELEVATION

A. M. KEMPER

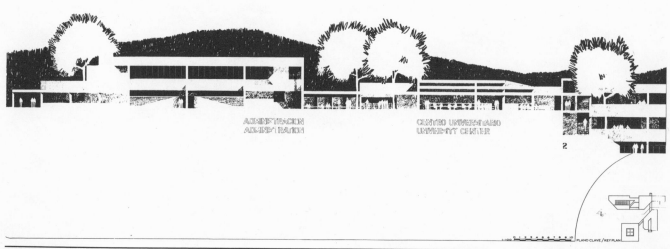

ADMINISTRACION
ADMINISTRATION

CENTRO UNIVERSITARIO
UNIVERSITY CENTER

PLANO CLAVE / KEY PLAN

GERD ERNST

DANIEL, MANN, JOHNSON, AND MENDENHALL **137**

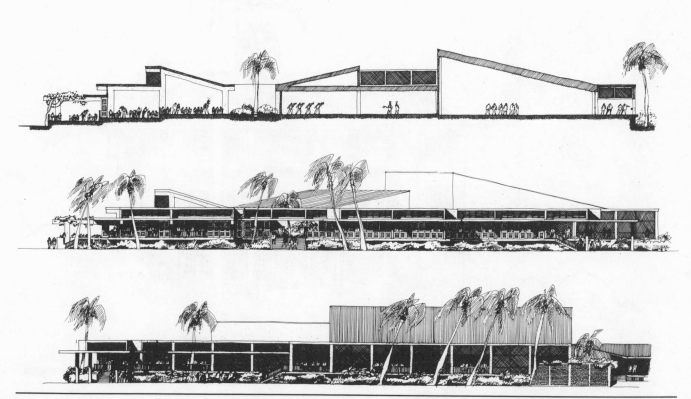

ESHERICK, HOMSEY, DODGE, AND DAVIS

138

ada smith mansion circa: 1900

·· AN EXAMPLE OF "CHICAGO SCHOOL" INFLUENCE ON SAN DIEGO ARCHITECTURE ·· CONTRIBUTIONS FOR RESTORATION SHOULD BE SENT TO "SAVE THE SMITH MANSION" @ SAVE OUR HERITAGE ORGANIZATION (S.O.H.O.) 225-1033

S. RESOR

S. RESOR

140

north elevation
1 E

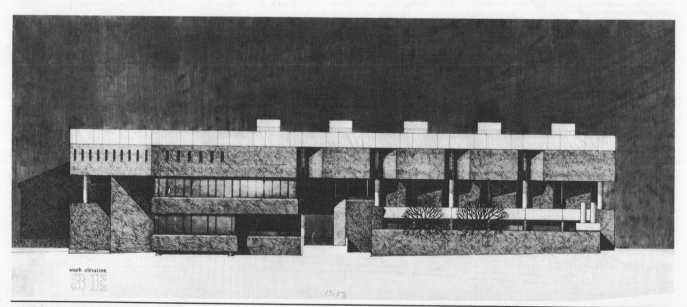

south elevation
3 E

MURRAY WHISNANT

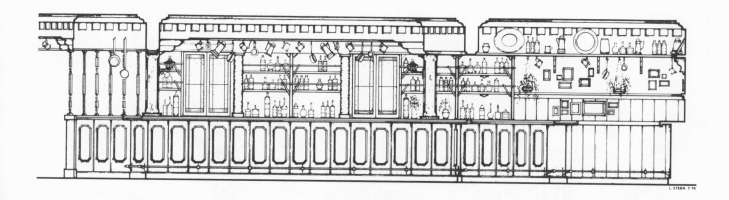

LEONARD A. STERN

MARTIN STERN, JR.

142

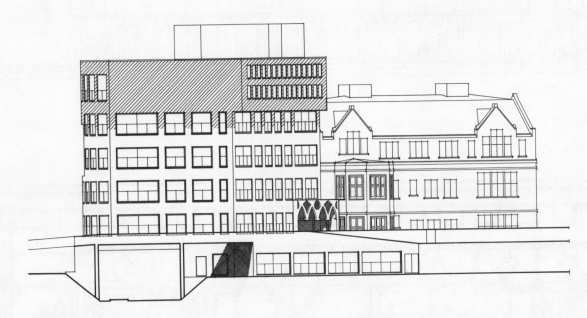

NORTHWEST ELEVATION

SOUTHWEST ELEVATION

VENTURI AND RAUCH

ELEVATION

CALLISTER, PAYNE, AND BISCHOFF

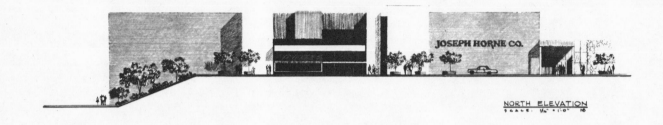

NORTH ELEVATION
SCALE: 1/16" = 1'-0"

EAST ELEVATION
SCALE: 1/16" = 1'-0"

144   MORGANELLI-HEUMANN-RUDD

ANSHEN AND ALLEN

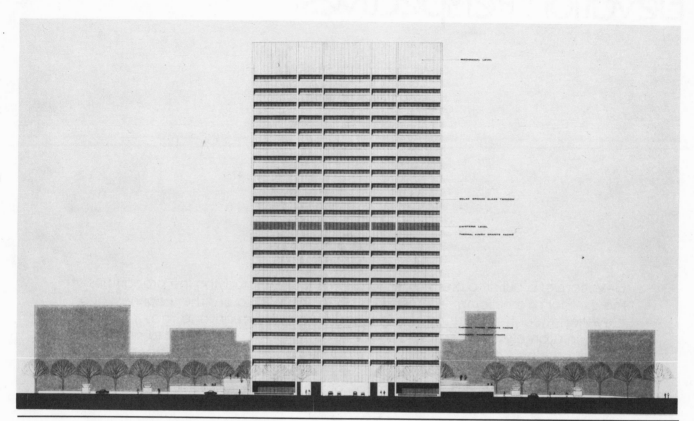

JOHN CARL WARNECKE AND PETERSON, CLARK **145**

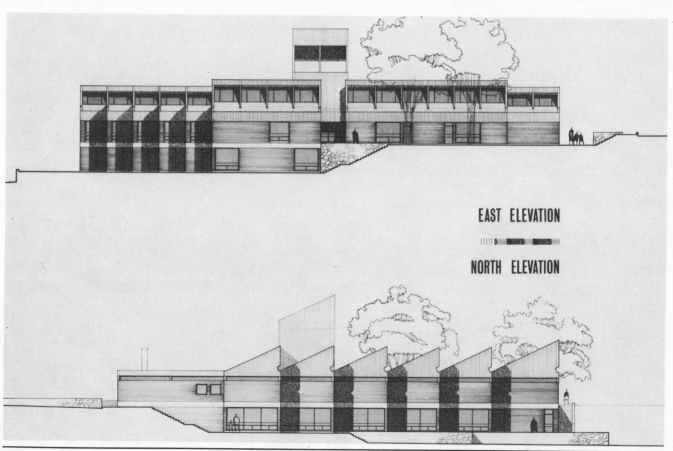

EAST ELEVATION

NORTH ELEVATION

EARL R. FLANSBURGH AND ASSOCIATES

Elevation Perspectives

9

Elevations of a building are the best drawings to use in studying the proportions of the exterior of a building, its masses, its openings, and so on. The weakness of an elevation though is the lack of depth indication. Although one may put some depth into an elevation by using shades and shadows, a fast way to produce a third dimension is to put the elevation into a "perspective." This is done quickly, requiring minimum skill and time, and is effective for both the designer as a study stage and for the client as a visualization of the building in its surroundings.

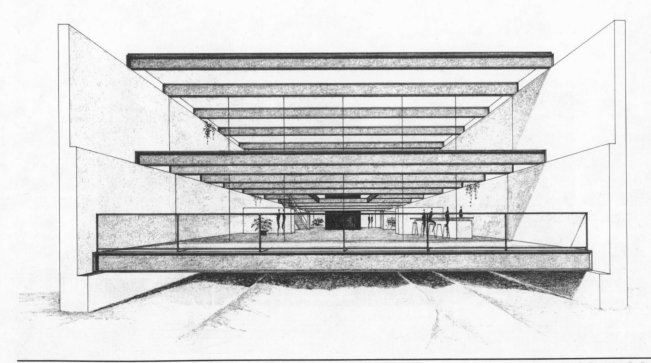

P. J. JACOBSON

CRAIG ELLWOOD ASSOCIATES

148 HARLAN GEORGESCO

HELMUT JACOBY   ARMAND BARTOS AND ASSOCIATES

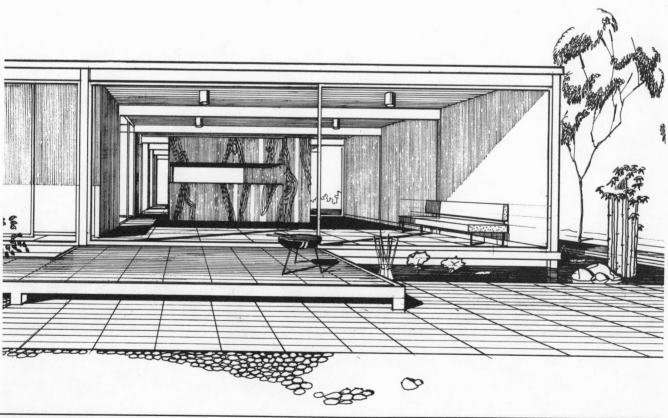

PIERRE KOENIG

150

CHARLES KANNER

151

RALPH RAPSON AND ASSOCIATES

152

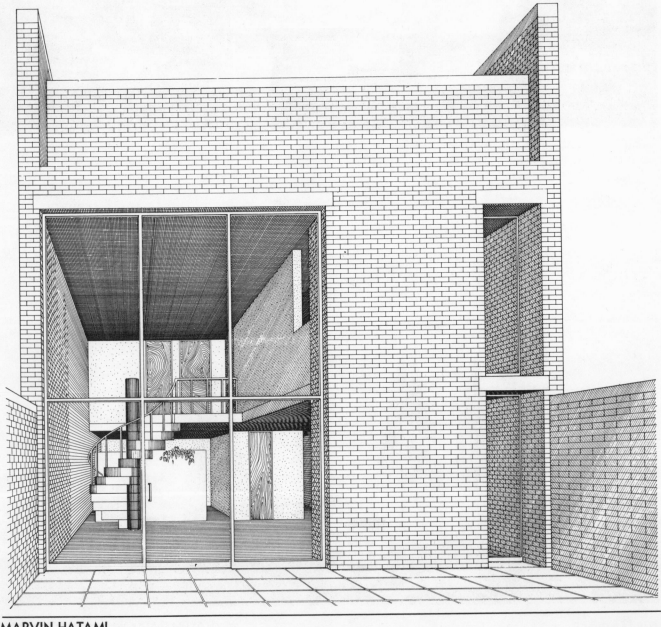

MARVIN HATAMI

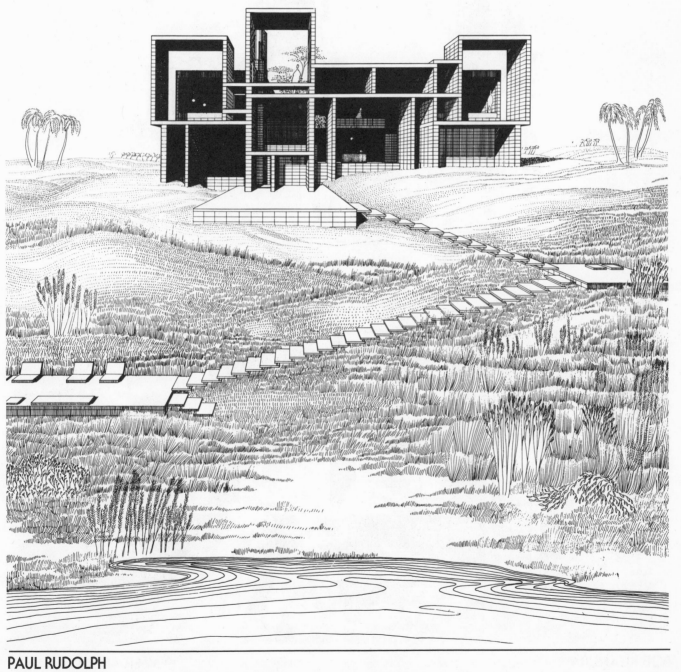

153

PAUL RUDOLPH

154

DAVID MORGAN

HAMBY, KENNERLY, SLOMANSON, AND SMITH

Interiors

10

The best way to draw architectural space is from within the space used by the inhabitants. By definition architectural space should be enclosed space, that is, defined space. Too many times architects present their buildings as if they were to be used only for walking around and viewing from afar. But to the client it is important how his building looks from the inside. The perspective sketch or "rendering" showing a space in more or less realistic fashion is a key document for explaining the design. Most architects make as few interior drawings as their budget permits. Many architects are, however, sensitive enough to draw the enclosed space.

GEORGE CARROL

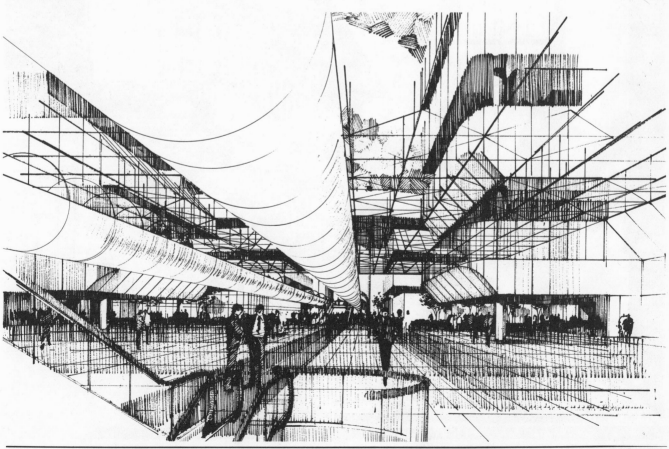

WELTON BECKET AND ASSOCIATES

R. KARLIS
FRED BASSETTI AND COMPANY

159

JACK BARKLEY

HELLMUTH, OBATA, AND KASSABAUM, INC.

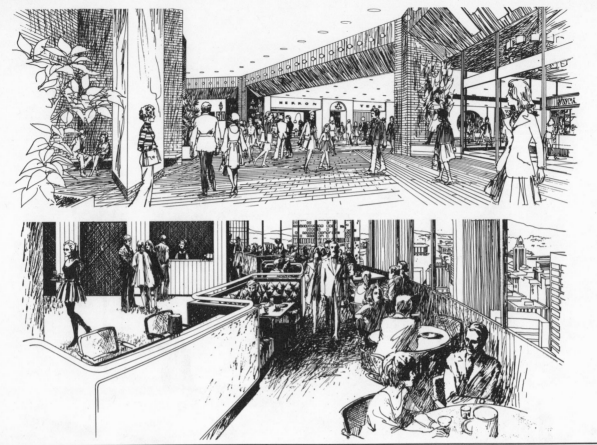

160 CARLOS DINIZ   CHARLES LUCKMAN ASSOCIATES

FRANCISCO ARAUJO   MAYER AND KANNER

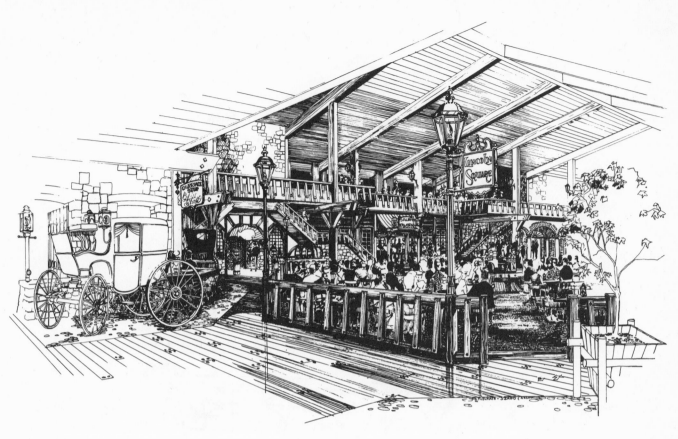

161

McERATH AND SZOBO

SHOJI SHIMIZU

ADRIAN WILSON ASSOCIATES

163

WILLIS H. MILLS, JR.

SMS ARCHITECTS

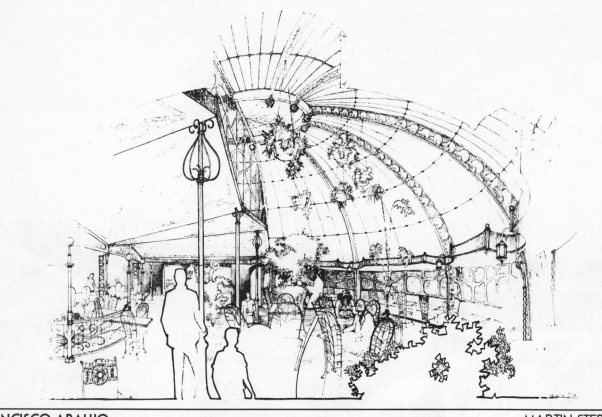

MARTIN STERN, JR.

HUGH STUBBINS AND ASSOCIATES

165

166

GEORGE CONLEY

HUGH STUBBINS AND ASSOCIATES

JACK BARKLEY

HELLMUTH, OBATA, AND KASSABAUM, INC. **167**

HUYGENS AND TAPPE INC.

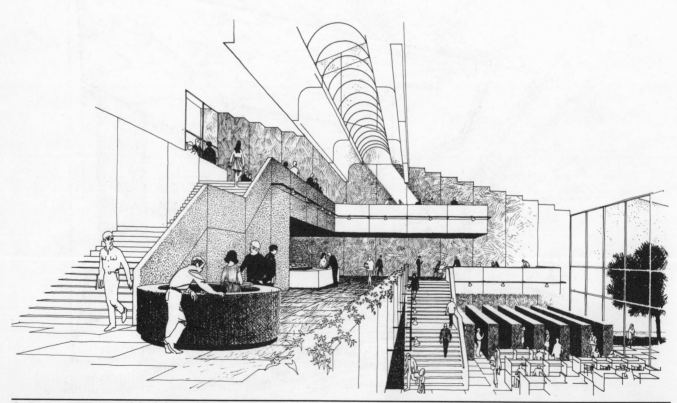

CARLOS DINIZ   HONNOLD, REIBSAMEN, AND REX

169

JACK BARKLEY

HELLMUTH, OBATA, AND KASSABAUM, INC.

170 CARLETON KOVELL

NARAMORE, BAIN, BRADY, AND JOHANSON

HELMUT JACOBY

I. M. PEI AND PARTNERS

171

WALTER GREUB

LANGDON AND WILSON

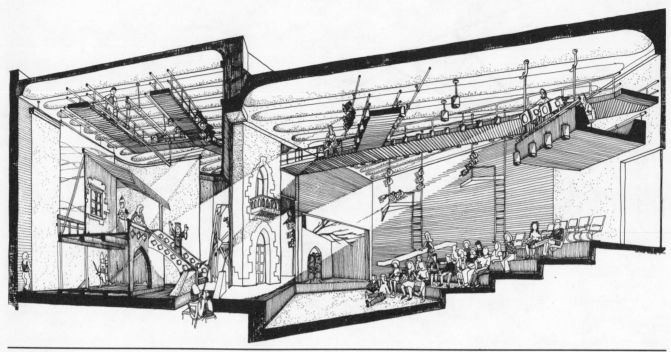

172 G. YOURKE

WARNER, BURNS, TOAN, LUNDE

GERALD K. LEE

ESHERICK, HOMSEY, DODGE, AND DAVIS

BOB KITAMURA

HONNOLD, REIBSAMEN, AND REX

174 CHRISTOPHER RIDDLE

CALLISTER AND PAYNE

DONALD REAY

DEMARS AND REAY

DONALD REED

JOHN C. WARNECKE AND ASSOCIATES

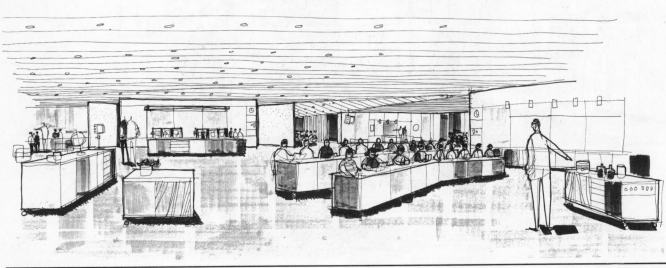

176 FRED LAPPIN DANIEL, MANN, JOHNSON, AND MENDENHALL

INGRID STOLLMAN WARNER, BURNS, TOAN, LUNDE

JAMES K. M. CHENG

BULL, FIELD, VOLKMANN, STOCKWELL

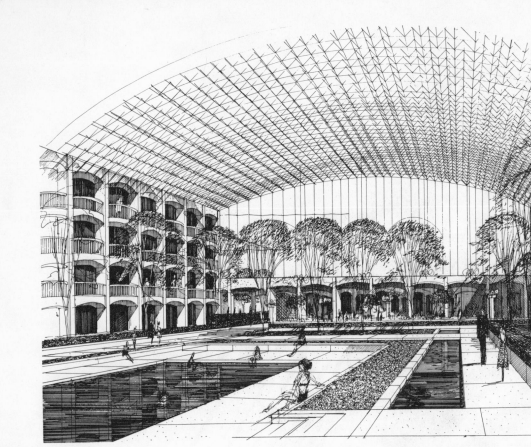

JOHN DESMOND

179

Partial Perspectives

11

Partial perspective is the most natural way of presenting or drawing space, for it is almost the way we actually see space. Seldom can the total building be seen at one glance, especially if it is very large. In the majority of actual life situations we usually see only the lower portion of the building as, for example, we approach the entry, or look through the lobby into the courtyard, or look from one space into another, through a window or doorway, and so on. Unfortunately as architects we too often avoid drawing partial perspectives. For a client, however, partial perspectives can be an exciting help during the design process for learning to understand and for feeling the building design develop.

CARLOS DINIZ   HONNOLD, REIBSAMEN, AND REX   181

O. DAHLSTRAND   JOHN C. WARNECKE AND ASSOCIATES

182 H. MORSE PAYNE

MICHAEL F. GEBHART   TAC

CHRISTOPHER RIDDLE

TERRY STEPHENS

CALLISTER AND PAYNE

184

DONALD A. REED

EARL R. FLANSBURGH AND ASSOCIATES

WALLACE, McHARG, ROBERTS, AND TODD

186

CENTRAL AXIS

OTTER WALK

PERRY, DEAN AND STEWART

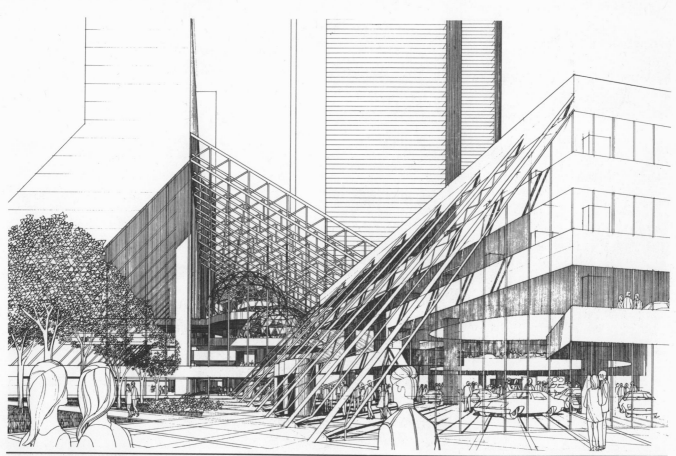

GEORGE CONLEY

HUGH STUBBINS AND ASSOCIATES

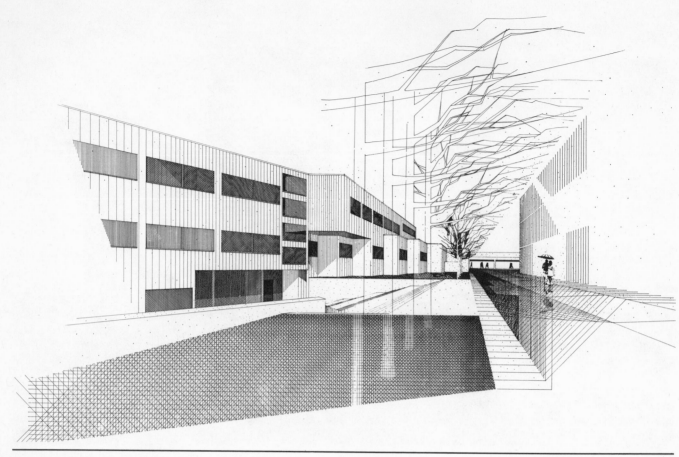

VENTURI AND RAUCH

A. QUINCY JONES

SARGENT, WEBSTER, CRENSHAW, AND FOLLEY 189

LEAVITT DUDLEY   DANIEL, MANN, JOHNSON, AND MENDENHALL

WILLIAM SIMONIUM

KAHN, KAPPE, LOTTERY

JACK BARKLEY

HELLMUTH, OBATA, AND KASSABAUM, INC. 191

HON-MING NG

MARQUIS AND STOLLER

192 DANIEL DWORSKY

DONALD REAY   **DEMARS AND REAY**

PETER GUMPEL

CAUDILL ROWLETT SCOTT 193

F. LYMAN

194

BOB KITAMURA

PRIEST, RICHMOND, WOLF AND ROSSI

PAUL RUDOLPH

BEN ALTHEN

GRUEN ASSOCIATES

DONALD A. REED

RONALD LOVE

PHILIP JOHNSON AND JOHN BURGEE

198 CARLOS DINIZ

WURSTER, BERNARDI AND EMMONS, INC.

H. MARTIN

D. SPECTER

DON WOODRUFF

ECKBO, DEAN, AUSTIN, AND WILLIAMS   199

LARRY MEREK

GRUZEN AND PARTNERS

CARLOS DINIZ

MINORU YAMASAKI

VAL THORTON

ALBERT C. MARTIN AND ASSOCIATES **201**

E. MANARTE

LEE HARRIS POMEROY

Special Drawings

12

As the occasion arises an architect may want to show a specific portion of his design either to his consultants or to his client. As with sketches the choice of drawing to show some special aspect of the design is personal. But the basic rule of clarity in presentation prevails. The following examples show the variety of techniques that may be used to emphasize these special drawings.

203

WALLACE, McHARG, ROBERTS, AND TODD

204

BRENT, GOLDMAN, ROBBINS & BOWN

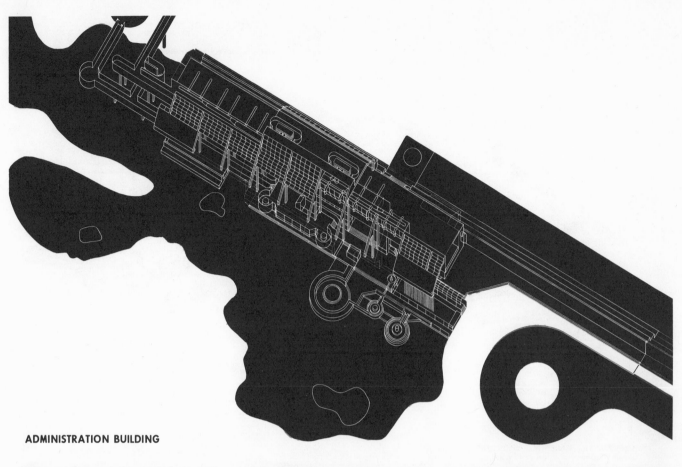

ADMINISTRATION BUILDING

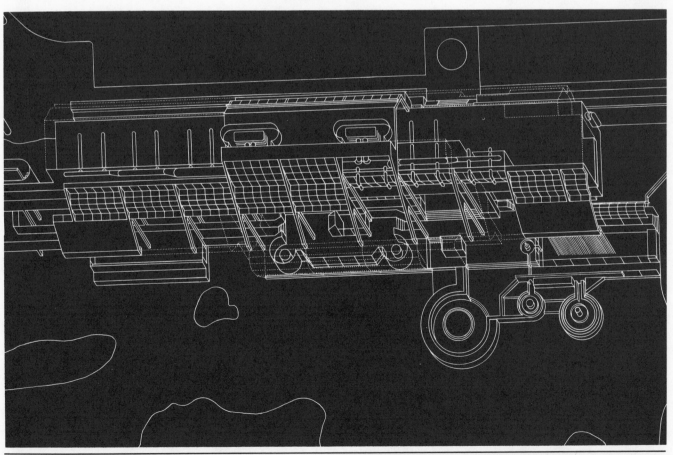

DANIEL, MANN, JOHNSON, AND MENDENHALL

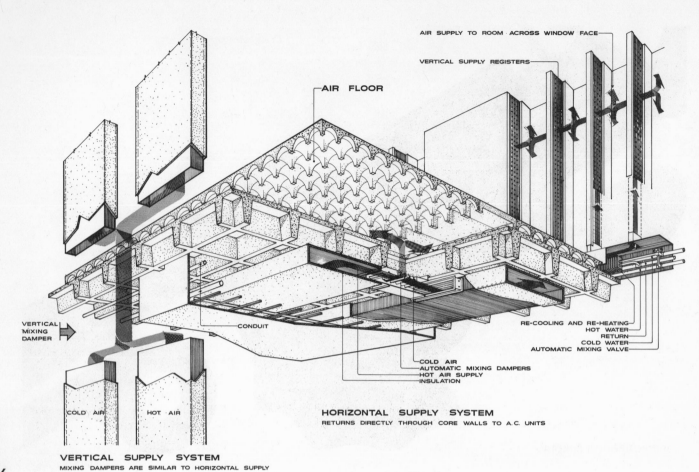

AIR SUPPLY TO ROOM ACROSS WINDOW FACE

VERTICAL SUPPLY REGISTERS

AIR FLOOR

VERTICAL
MIXING
DAMPER

CONDUIT

RE-COOLING AND RE-HEATING
HOT WATER
RETURN
COLD WATER
AUTOMATIC MIXING VALVE

COLD AIR
AUTOMATIC MIXING DAMPERS
HOT AIR SUPPLY
INSULATION

COLD AIR   HOT AIR

HORIZONTAL SUPPLY SYSTEM
RETURNS DIRECTLY THROUGH CORE WALLS TO A.C. UNITS

VERTICAL SUPPLY SYSTEM
MIXING DAMPERS ARE SIMILAR TO HORIZONTAL SUPPLY

206

PERSPECTIVE SECTION

FLOOR PLAN
SCALE: 1/8" = 1'-0"

A. QUINCY JONES AND ASSOCIATES

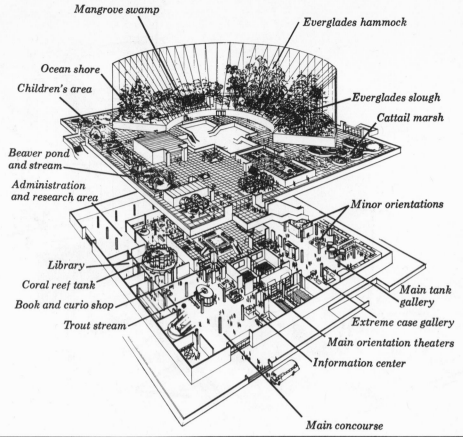

Mangrove swamp

Everglades hammock

Ocean shore

Children's area

Everglades slough

Cattail marsh

Beaver pond
and stream

Administration
and research area

Minor orientations

Library

Coral reef tank

Book and curio shop

Trout stream

Main tank
gallery

Extreme case gallery

Main orientation theaters

Information center

Main concourse

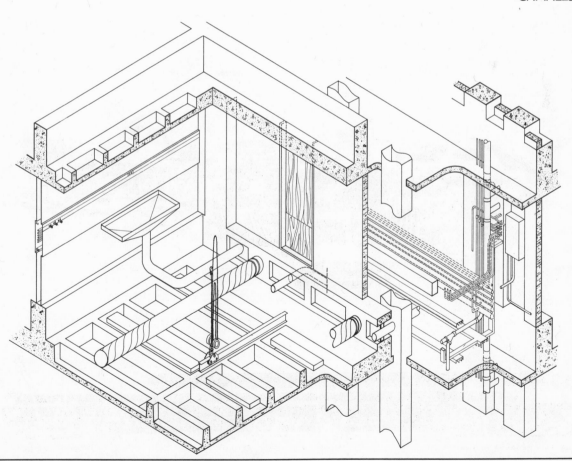

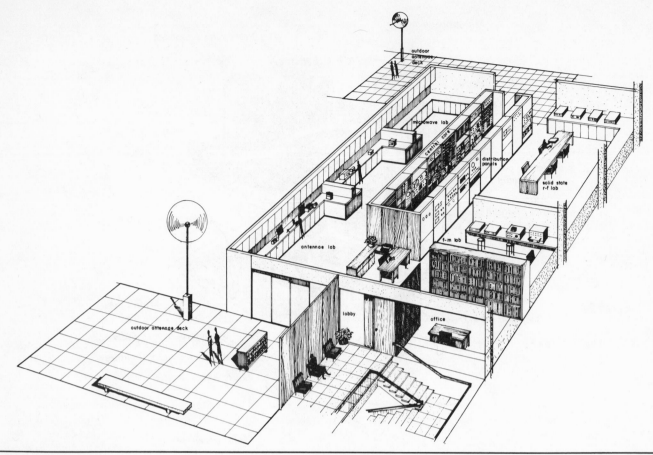

208 JOHN DESMOND

VIEW OF RESTAURANT & BAR FROM POOL TERRACE

EAST ELEVATION OF RESTAURANT LOOKING FROM POOL

GERALD K. LEE   **ESHERICK, HOMSEY, DODGE, AND DAVIS**

GERALD K. LEE

ESHERICK, HOMSEY, DODGE, AND DAVIS

Isometrics

13

Iso means "equal." An isometric is a drawing showing equal exposure to each of the three planes of an octagonal object. Moreover the three dimensions (axes) are at 120 degrees from each other at an outside corner; the three dimensions are also at the same scale. Isometrics are easily constructed by using a 30/60 right triangle and are mostly used for examining spatial structure. Exploded views are frequently used to explain complete details, traffic patterns, or space relationships.

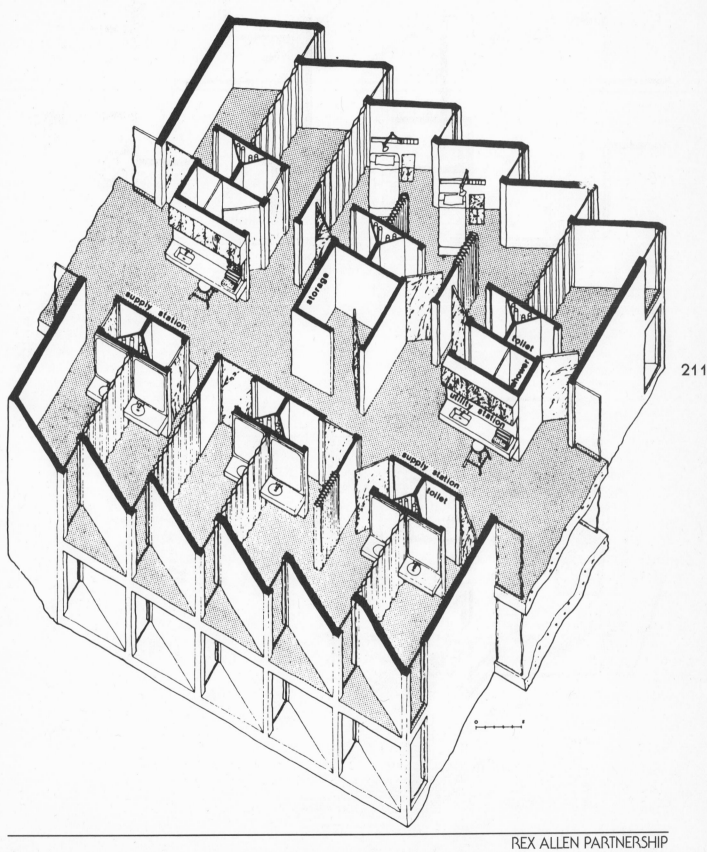

supply station

storage

toilet

shower

utility station

supply station

toilet

211

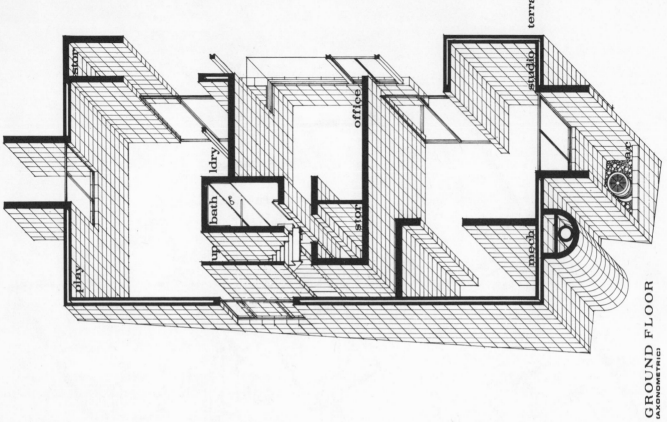

stor

ldry

bath

up

play

office

stor

studio

terrace

a.c.

mech

GROUND FLOOR
(AXONOMETRIC)

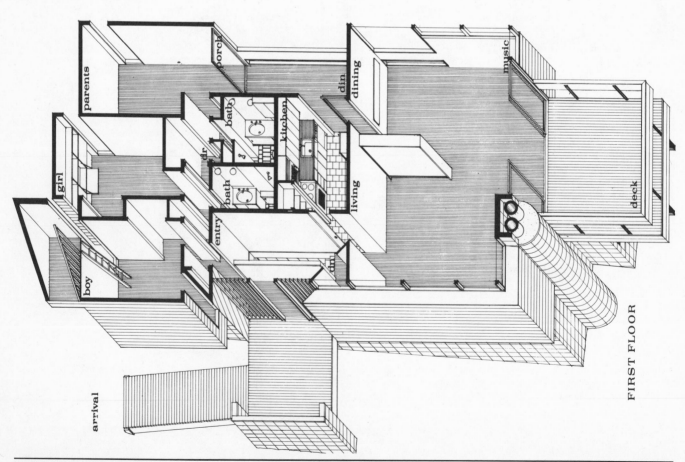

parents

girl

boy

dr

bath

entry

bath

porch

kitchen

din

dining

living

music

deck

arrival

FIRST FLOOR

MURRAY WHISNANT

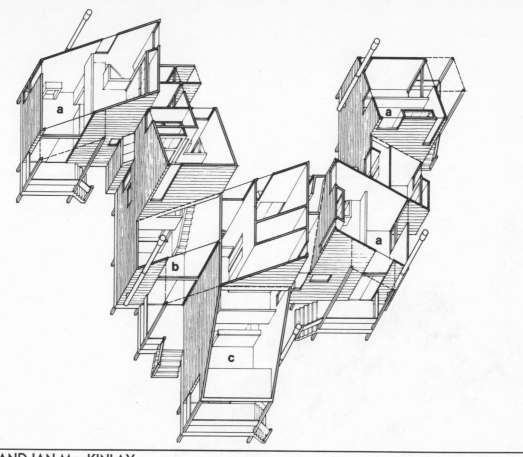

HENRIK BULL AND IAN MacKINLAY

213

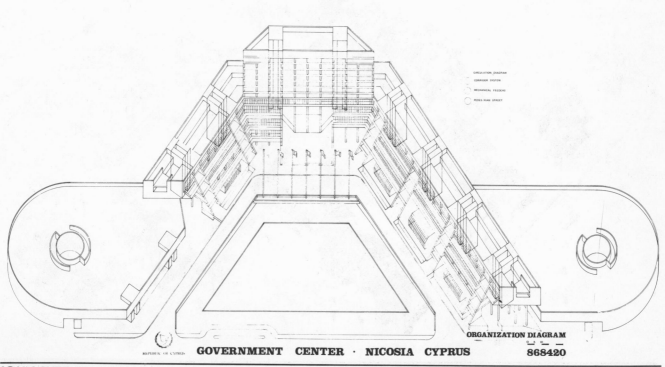

CIRCULATION DIAGRAM
CORRIDOR SYSTEM
MECHANICAL FEEDERS
PEDESTRIAN STREET

ORGANIZATION DIAGRAM

REPUBLIC OF CYPRUS **GOVERNMENT CENTER · NICOSIA CYPRUS** 868420

JOHN SHEEHY

TAC

214

RAMALDO GIURGOLA

MITCHELL/GIURGOLA ASSOCIATES

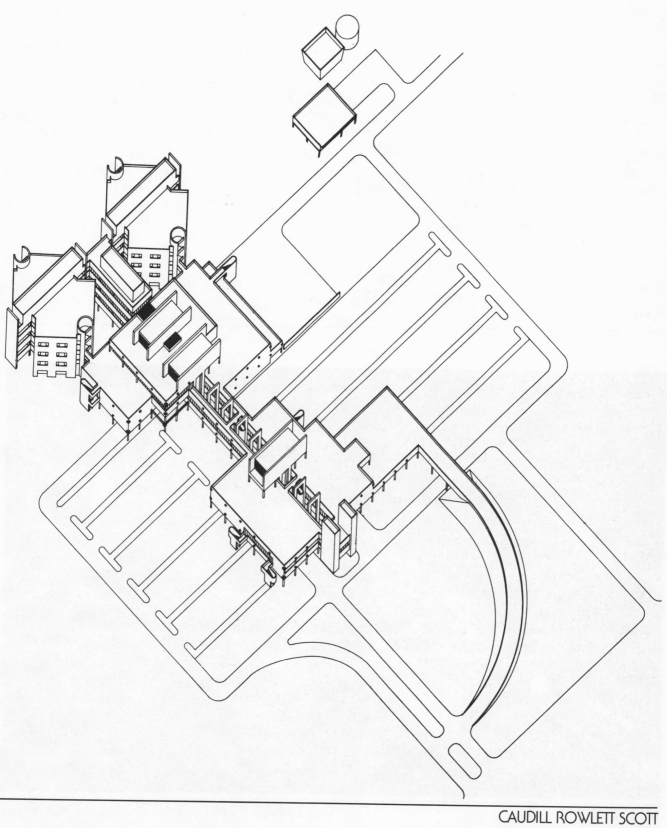

215

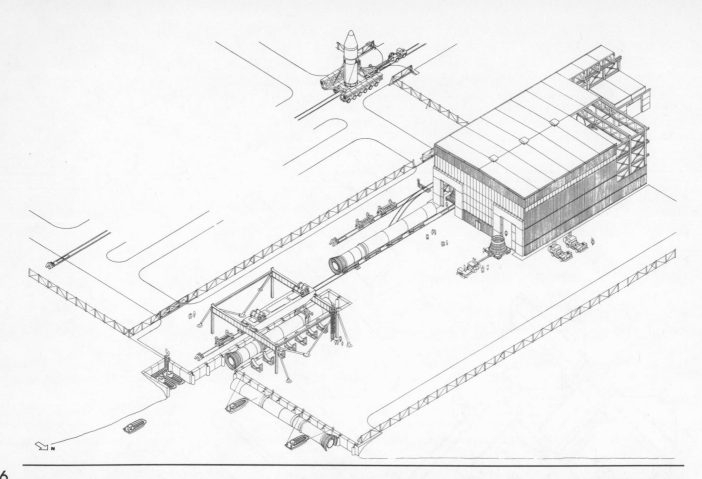

N

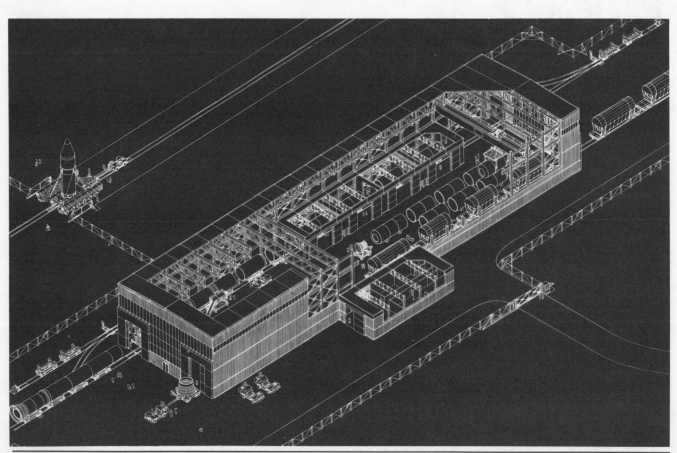

ALBERTO BERTOL

DANIEL, MANN, JOHNSON, AND MENDENHALL

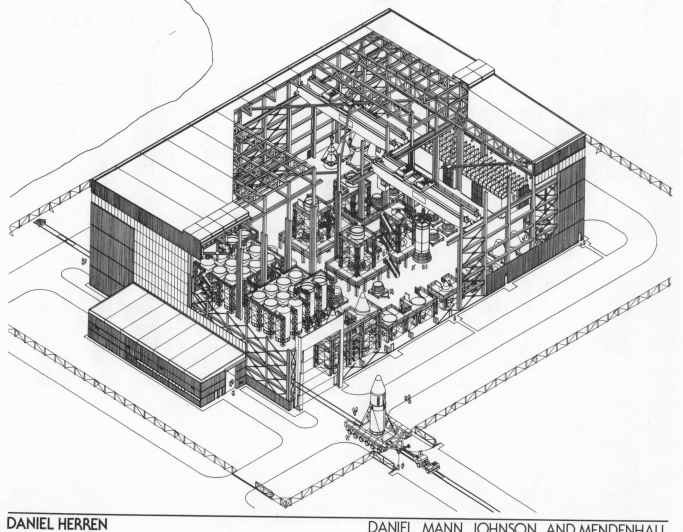

217

DANIEL HERREN

DANIEL, MANN, JOHNSON, AND MENDENHALL

218

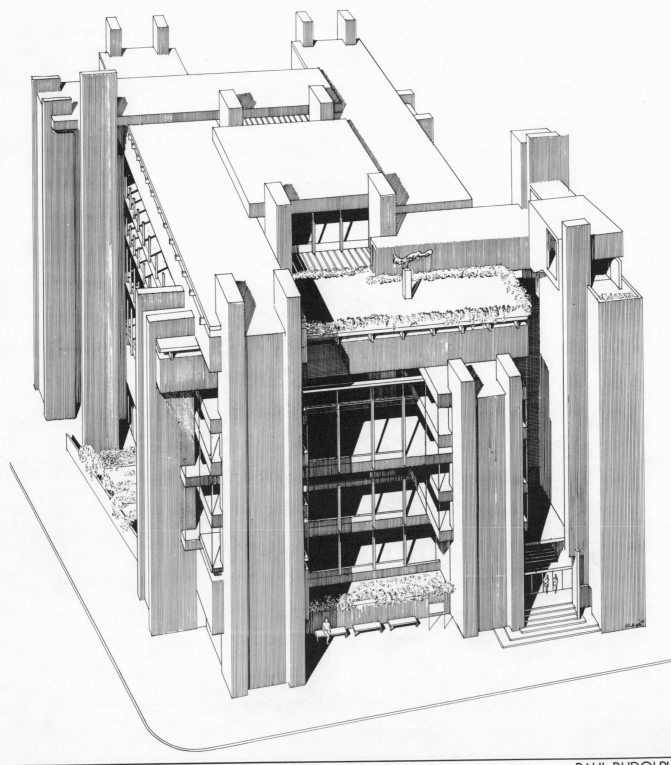

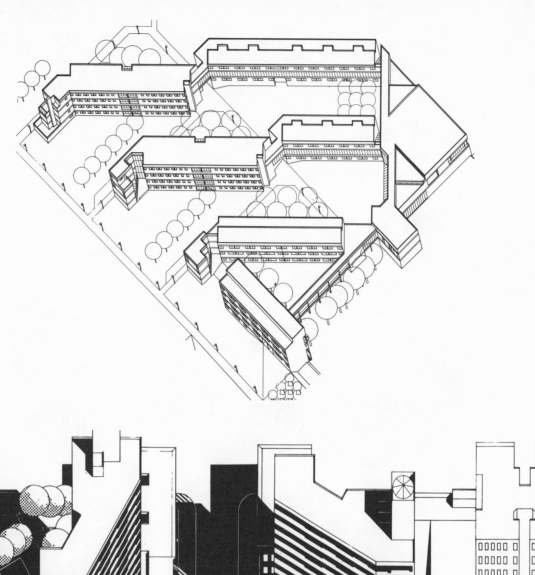

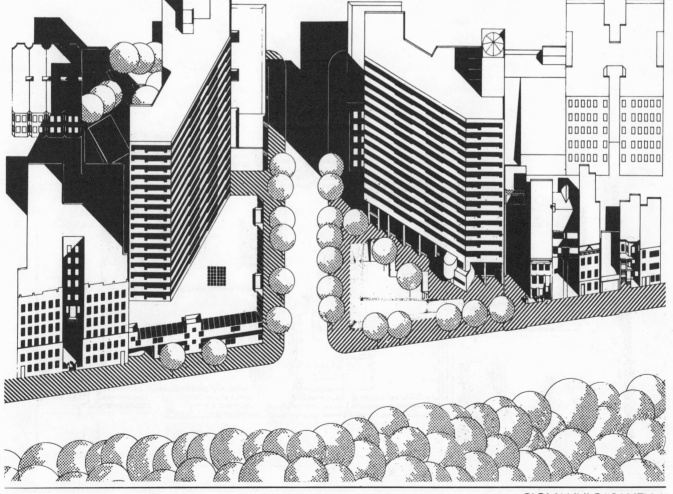

GIOVANNI PASANELLA

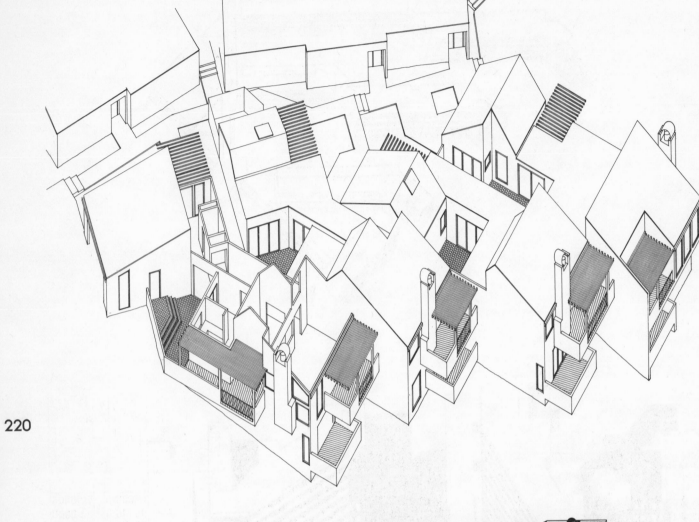

220

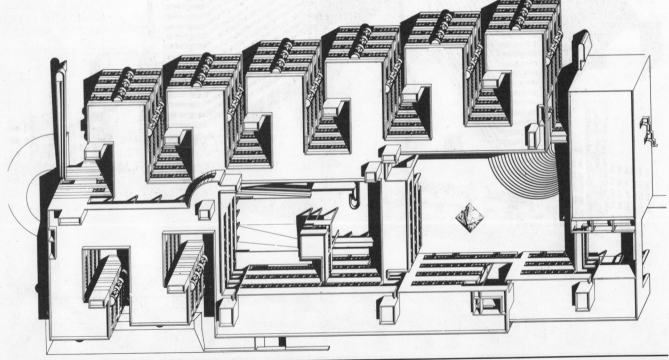

MacKINLAY AND WINNACKER

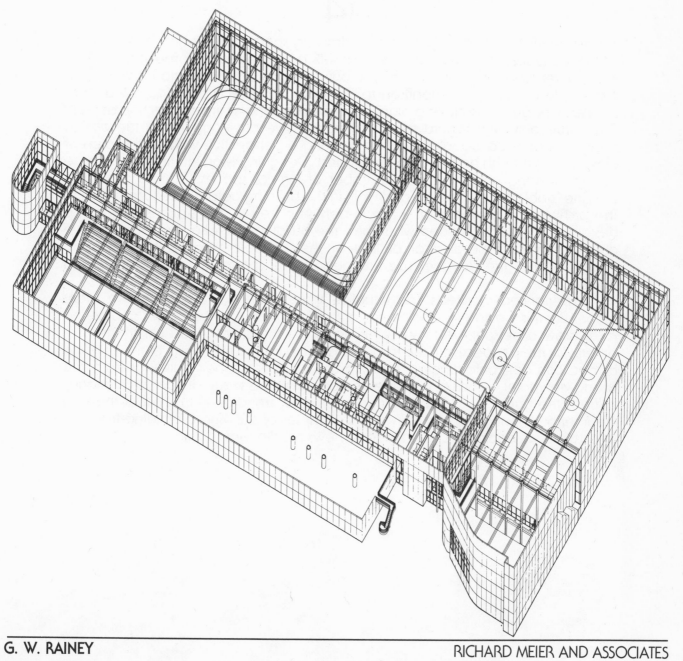

G. W. RAINEY

RICHARD MEIER AND ASSOCIATES

Perspectives

14

Perspective is the most natural way of drawing space, for it is how one actually perceives space. The perspective is what sells a building to a prospective client. It is, however, a laborious way to show a building. The plan, elevation, and section are simple to draw in comparison to drawing a perspective. In fact, to draw a perspective, one must have a plan, an elevation, and at times a section as well. This is true only with regard to a final perspective drawing. During the design stages the architect doodles a lot by drawing a perspective without the plan or elevation, although he has both in his mind. Designing is an intellectual exercise of experiencing a nearly infinite number of interior spaces. This is indeed the designer's obligation — to live and walk in the building before it becomes reality. The architectural presentation is the in-between step — the stage just after the designer's mind has decided what form the building will take. He must then be able to express to the client an outlook on the probable building. It is important, therefore, that the designer use the perspective constantly during the design stages.

Experienced architects can visualize three-dimensional space from plans alone. But this is a time-saving device only for himself. At one point or another he must draw a perspective to show his design to the client, juror, committee, or others, for the perspective is the image that is as close to the reality of the building as one can get. Unfortunately many architects present their buildings from the wrong viewpoint — such as from the treetop across the street, or from an airplane, or from the gutter — all in one glorious full-color smudge — instead of showing the interior or enclosed space. Typical examples of showing a building from an impossible viewpoint are found in most news media reproductions.

223

224

ANSHEN AND ALLEN

225

ANSHEN AND ALLEN

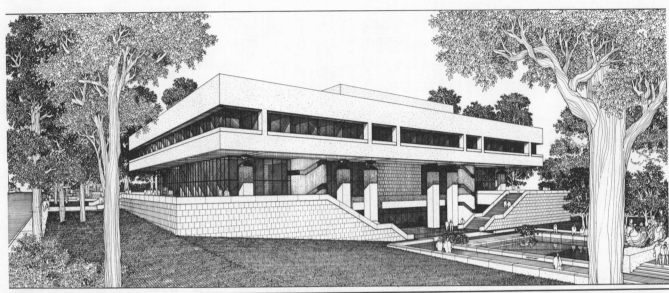

226 KEMP MOONEY

STEVENS AND WILKINSON

TOM MURPHY

REX ALLEN PARTNERSHIP

LOUIS ANGELIKIS

228

EDWARD DURELL STONE

ADRIAN WILSON ASSOCIATES   229

FRANK NEMETH   RALPH RAPSON AND ASSOCIATES

HEATON RESIDENCE

230 BOB KITAMURA

KEMPER AND ASSOCIATES

EFRAM OLIVER

FERENDINO, GRAFTON, SPILLIS, CANDELA

DAN NICHOLL

WILLIAM SIMONIUM

KAHN, KAPPE, LOTTERY

232

CARLOS DINIZ

CHARLES LUCKMAN ASSOCIATES

GERALD K. LEE

ESHERICK, HOMSEY, DODGE, AND DAVIS 233

JAMES K. M. CHENG

BULL, FIELD, VOLKMANN, STOCKWELL

234

GERALD K. LEE   MARVIN E. GOODY, JOHN M CLANCY AND ASSOCIATES

235

BARRY ZAUSS

GRUEN ASSOCIATES

236   JOHN DESMOND

KAMNITZER/MARKS AND PARTNERS

TERRY STEPHENS

CALLISTER AND PAYNE 237

PETER GUMPEL

CAUDILL ROWLETT SCOTT

McELRATH AND SZOBO

JACK BARKLEY

HELLMUTH, OBATA, AND KASSABAUM

240

LARRY PERRON (LUTZ ASSOCIATES)   MARCEL BREUER AND TICIAN PARACHRISTOU

LOUIS GADAL

PAUL RUDOLPH

JOHN CARL WARNECKE AND ASSOCIATES

R. BENNETT AND KEN SAILOR

FROST ASSOCIATES

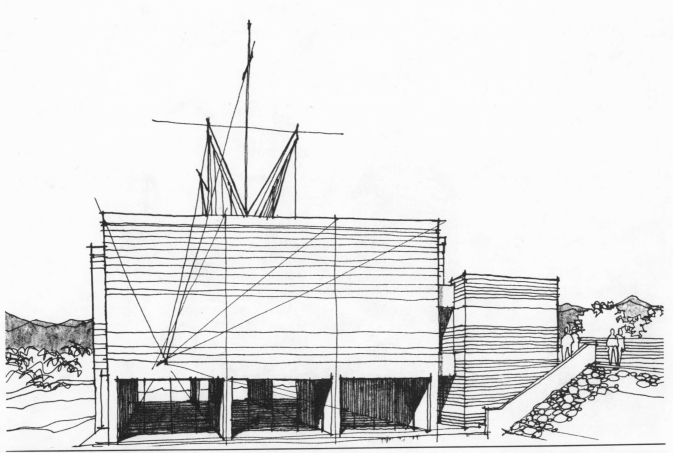

WILLIAM KIRBY LOCKARD

244 SHOJI SHIMIZU

ADRIAN WILSON ASSOCIATES

JAMES K. M. CHENG

BULL, FIELD, VOLKMANN, STOCKWELL

PHILIP JOHNSON AND JOHN BURGEE   **245**

DESMOND-MIREMONT-BURKS

246 MICHAEL F. GEBHART

TAC

T. LARSON AND J. SHEEHY

TAC

RALPH RAPSON AND ASSOCIATES

248 DRAWING

COMPLETED BUILDING

LOMAX ASSOCIATES

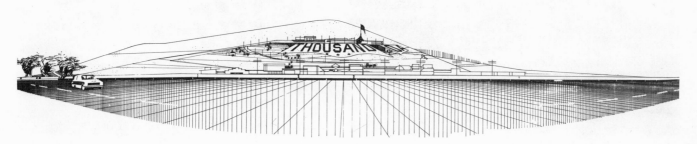

249

VENTURI AND RAUCH

250

M. D. MAHLER

KIRK-WALLACE-McKINLEY

JOHN S. BOLLES

MITCHELL/GIURGOLA ASSOCIATES

252 MARK DeNALOVY ROZVADOVSKI   LEE HARRIS POMEROY

SHOJI SHIMIZU   ADRIAN WILSON ASSOCIATES

WALTER GREUB

LANGDON AND WILSON

Aerial Perspectives

15

Aerial perspectives are far too popular in my opinion, since we seldom see our buildings from the air, especially from a level so low that details are recognizable. Unless we are designing a very large project, aerial perspectives should be only complementary to eye-level perspectives. There are, however, occasions when aerial perspectives are justified, as some of the following samples show.

254

MARK DeNALOVY ROZVADOVSKI

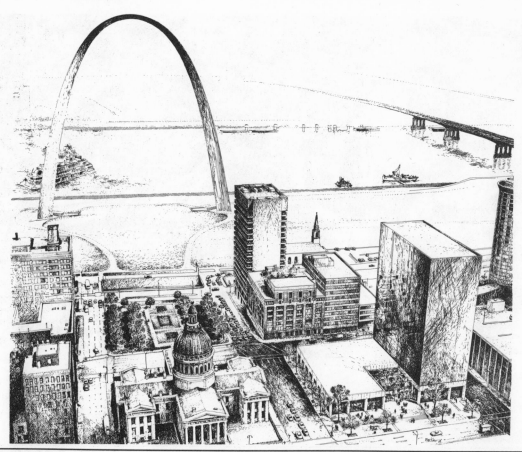

JACK BARKLEY

HELLMUTH, OBATA AND KASSABAUM

CARLOS DINIZ

ESHERICK, HOMSEY, DODGE, AND DAVIS

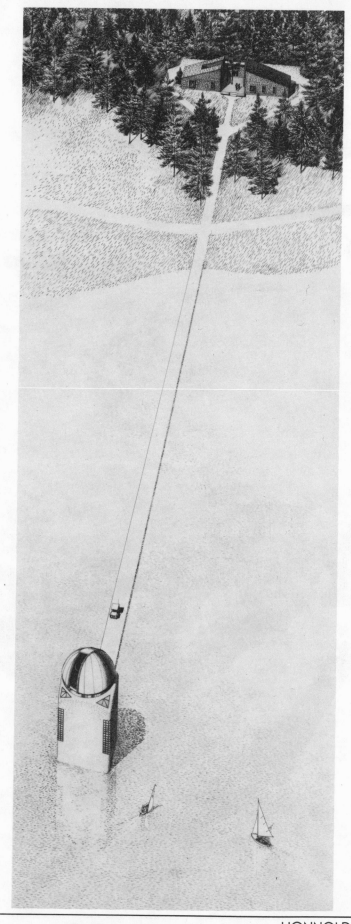

257

P. NICHOLAS

MARQUIS AND STOLLER

FRANCISCO ARAUJO

MAYER AND KANNER **259**

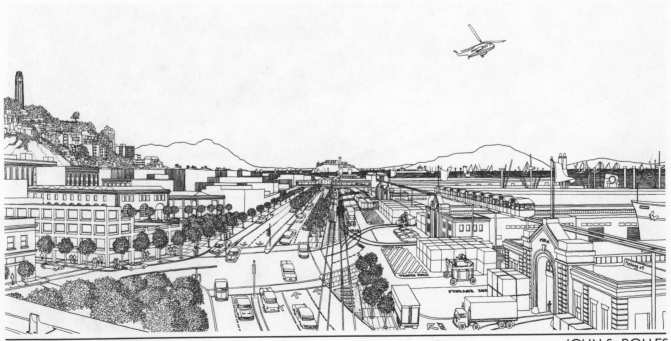

CHARLES O. RUSHING, JR.

JOHN S. BOLLES

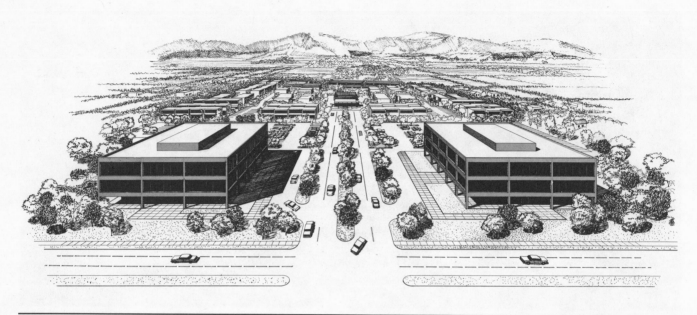

260

FRANCISCO ARAUJO

E. J. SAMANIEGO

D. SLOAN

261

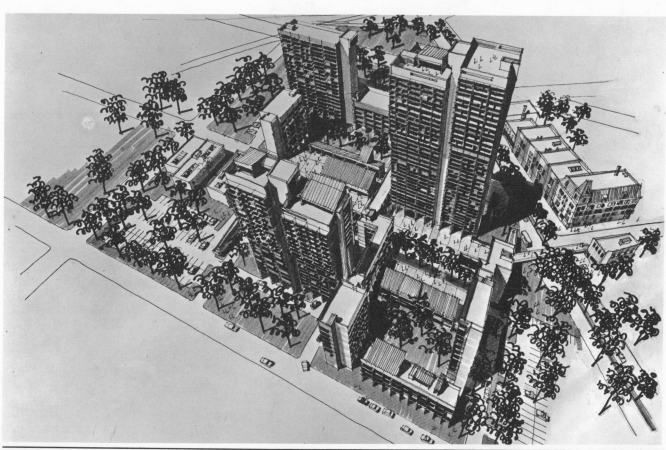

FRANK NEMETH

RALPH RAPSON AND ASSOCIATES

262 WALTER GREUB

LANGDON AND WILSON

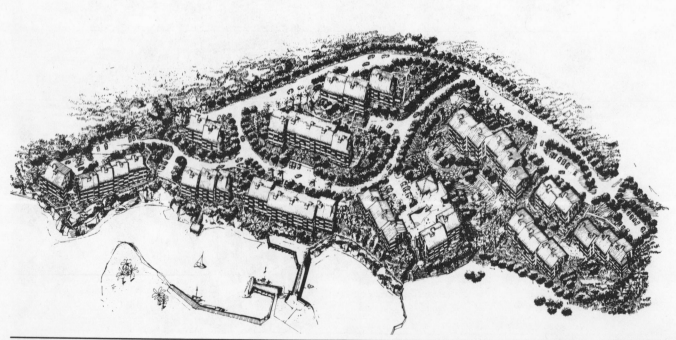

GERALD K. LEE

ESHERICK, HOMSEY, DODGE, AND DAVIS

PAUL RUDOLPH

JACK BARKLEY   HELLMUTH, OBATA AND KASSABAUM

KEM GARDENS   BRENT, GOLDMAN, ROBBINS & BOWN

R. BENNETT AND K. SAILOR

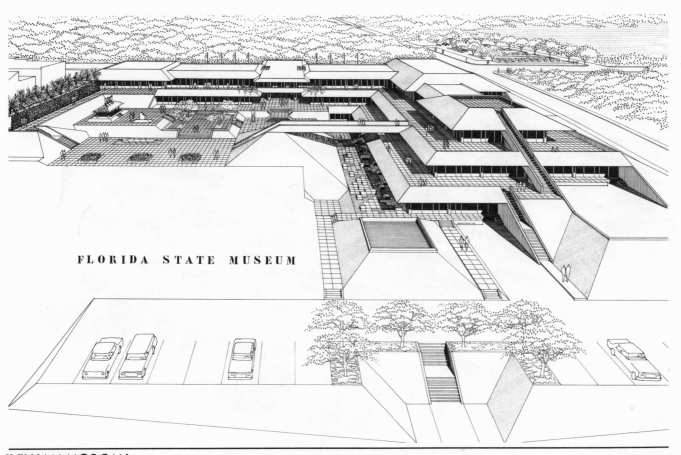

FLORIDA STATE MUSEUM

WILLIAM MORGAN

266 O. DAHLSTRAND

JOHN CARL WARNECKE AND ASSOCIATES

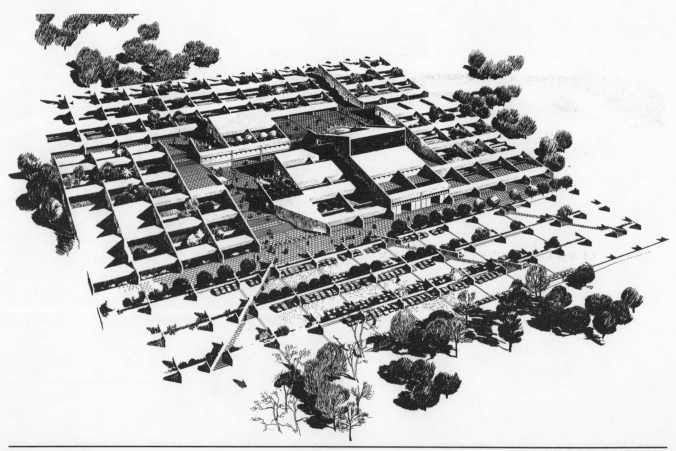

CARLOS DINIZ

HONNOLD, REIBSAMEN AND REX

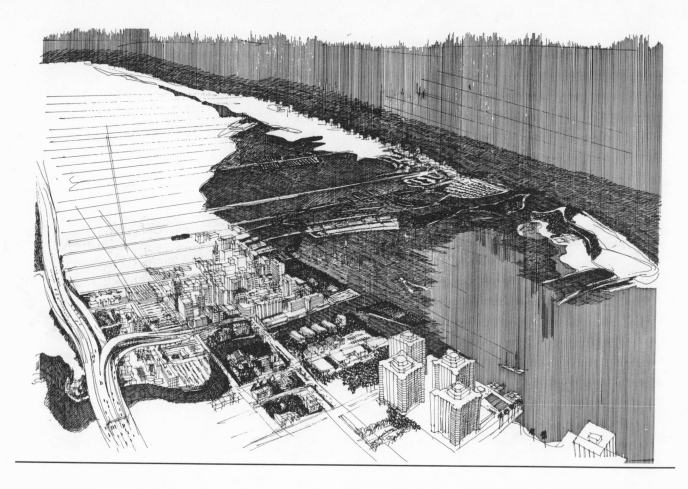

JOHN DESMOND   DESMOND-MIREMONT-BURKS

HUGH BROWNING

EARL R. FLANSBURGH AND ASSOCIATES

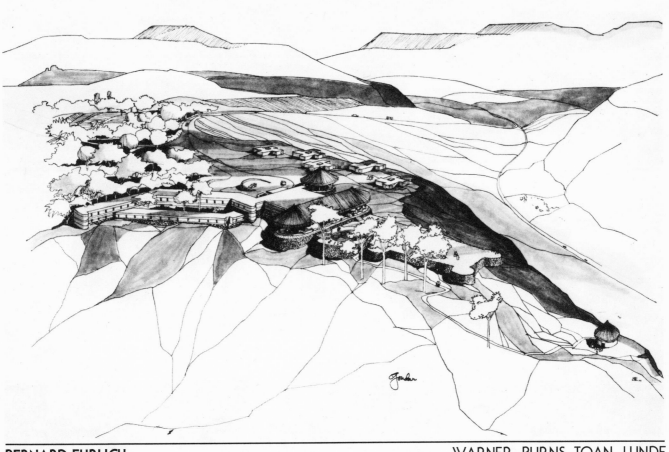

BERNARD EHRLICH

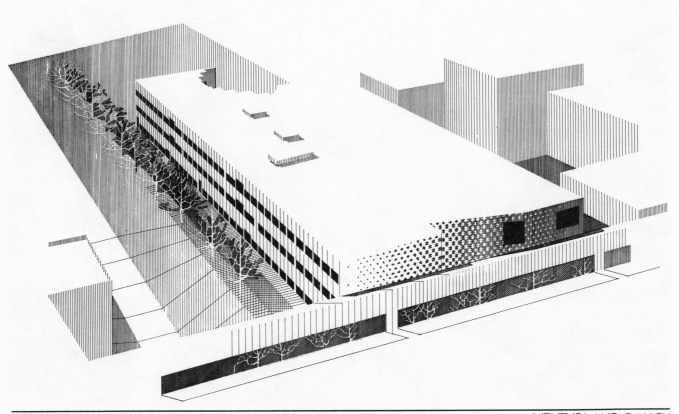

VENTURI AND RAUCH

TERRY STEPHENS   CALLISTER AND PAYNE

TERRY STEPHENS

CALLISTER AND PAYNE

Special Effects

16

This exciting section shows various special ways of presenting buildings. Few of us architects show our buildings at night (when artificially lighted) or show them covered and surrounded by snow. For certain specific jobs, however, it is important to show the building in this special way.

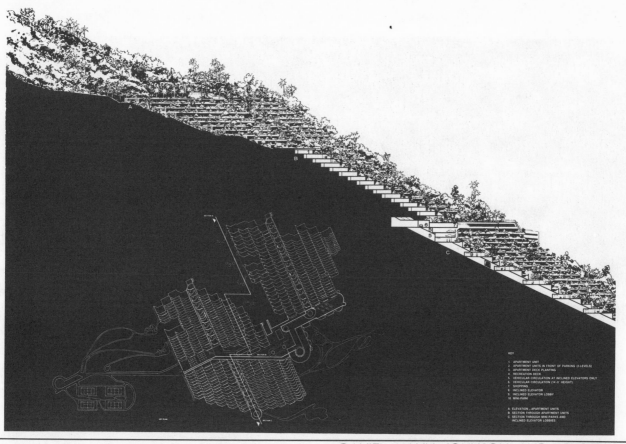

KEY
1. APARTMENT UNIT
2. APARTMENT UNITS IN FRONT OF PARKING (3 LEVELS)
3. APARTMENT DECK PLANTING
4. RECREATION DECK
5. VEHICULAR CIRCULATION AT INCLINED ELEVATORS ONLY
6. VEHICULAR CIRCULATION (14'-0 HEIGHT)
7. SHOPPING
8. INCLINED ELEVATOR
9. INCLINED ELEVATOR LOBBY
10. MINI-PARK

A. ELEVATION—APARTMENT UNITS
B. SECTION THROUGH APARTMENT UNITS
C. SECTION THROUGH MINI-PARKS AND
   INCLINED ELEVATOR LOBBIES

274 HARVEY FERRERO

LOUIS REDSTONE & ASSOCIATES

TOM AIDALA

DeMARS AND WELLS

ANNE KNORR

CORLETT AND SPACKMAN 275

J. DE QUESADA

HERTZKA AND KNOWLES

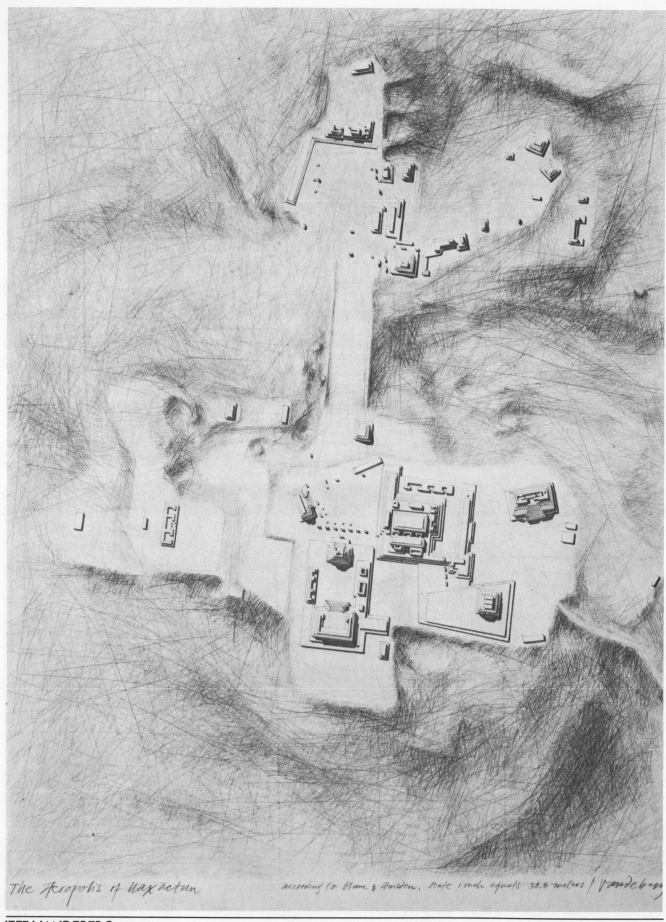

The Acropolis of Uaxactun   according to Blom & Ansden, scale 1 inch equals 38.8 meters / Vandeberg

JEFF VANDEBERG

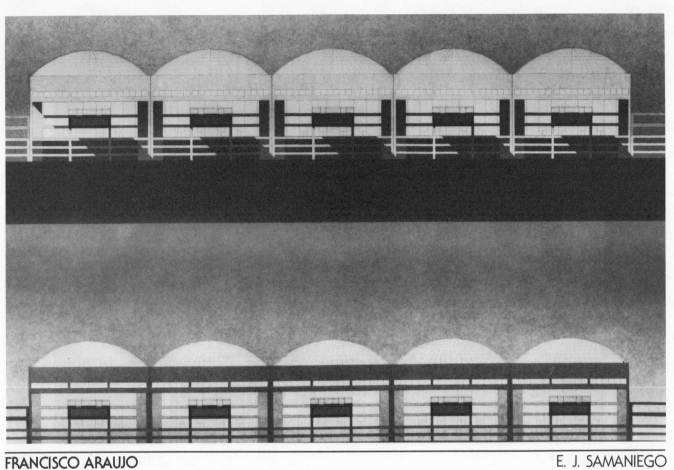

FRANCISCO ARAUJO

E. J. SAMANIEGO **277**

HUGH STUBBINS AND ASSOCIATES

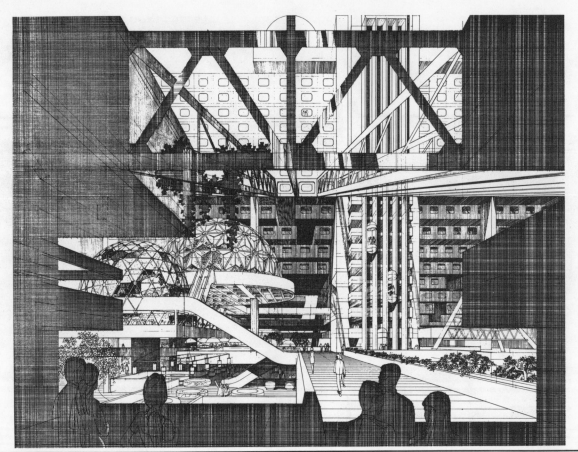

278 GEORGE CONLEY

HUGH STUBBINS AND ASSOCIATES

RICHARD PAYNE

CAUDILL ROWLETT SCOTT

HERB GREENE

THOMAS LARSON

280

281

BRENT, GOLDMAN, ROBBINS & BOWN

A. N. D'AVANZO

THE EGGERS PARTNERSHIP

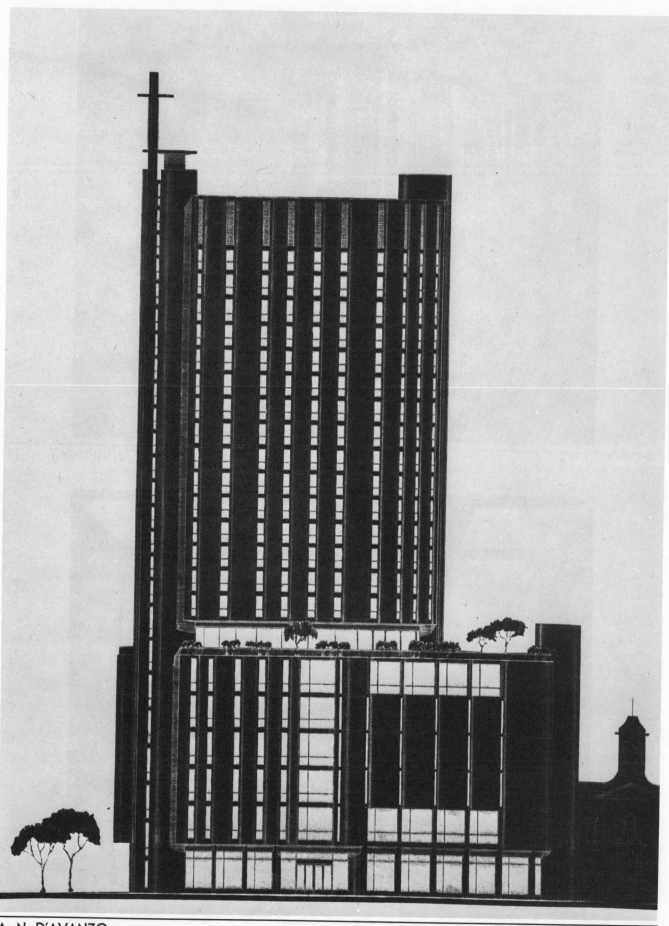

A. N. D'AVANZO

THE EGGERS PARTNERSHIP

ANSHEN AND ALLEN

CHARLES EAMES

285

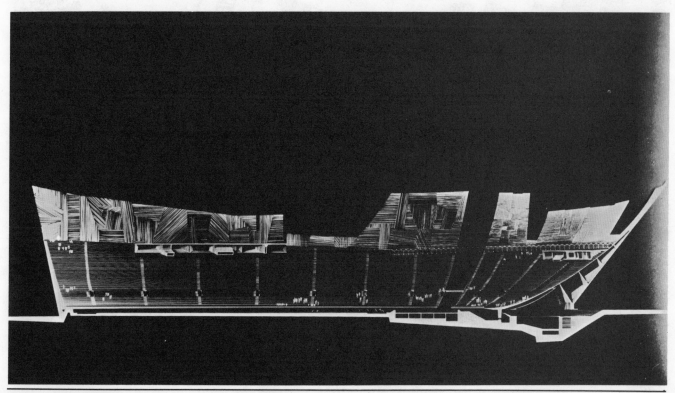

T. M. JANOWSKI

RICE AND ENGELBRECHT

286

GERD ERNST

DANIEL, MANN, JOHNSON, AND MENDENHALL

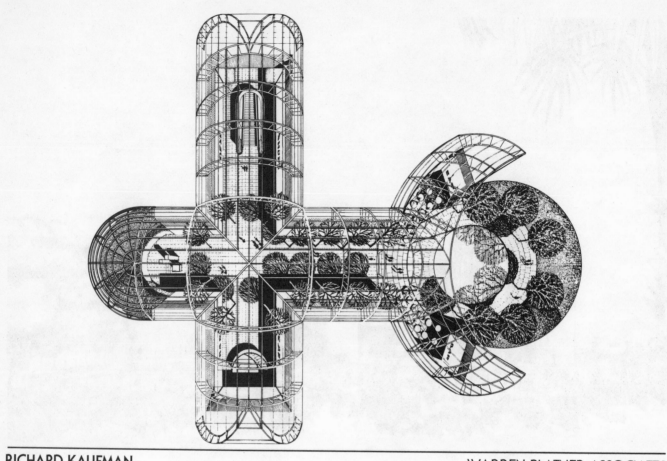

WARREN PLATNER ASSOCIATES

S. RESOR

SAM CARSON   HONNOLD, REIBSAMEN, AND REX   **289**

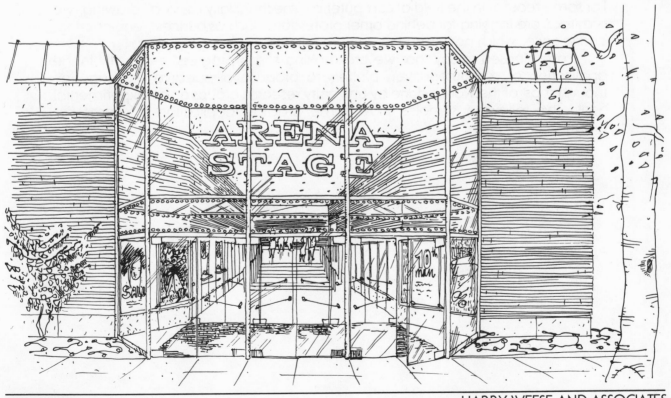

BEN WEESE   HARRY WEESE AND ASSOCIATES

Computer Drawings

17

Good drafting is a tedious process. We all know that, eventually, it will be replaced by machines, but so far this has not taken place. Large engineering offices already use some machines, in particular, the X–Y plotter or drum plotter. These machines are excellent tools for designing large industrial complexes, refinery plants, and so forth.

These same offices also use "photo-engineered" drawings, wherein actual screened photographs of the surroundings or detailed scaled models of new construction are reproduced on drafting film. Plastic pencils have been developed that can be washed off time and time again without wearing out the film (paper). Neither of these techniques is yet easily adaptable to the complex problems of designing buildings in our cities.

No doubt the capability of producing automated drawings exists, but few architects have tackled the problem of making them more meaningful or useful. For some reason, in the field of computer or "mechanically assisted" drawing, we architects are lagging far behind other professions, such as business, engineering, and science, which have gone through revolutionary changes.

I am pleased to say that we are making some progress, especially in the application of computer-driven plotters to produce perspective drawings, although most of the work is done by university research groups on an experimental basis. The following samples show some practical applications of computer graphics.

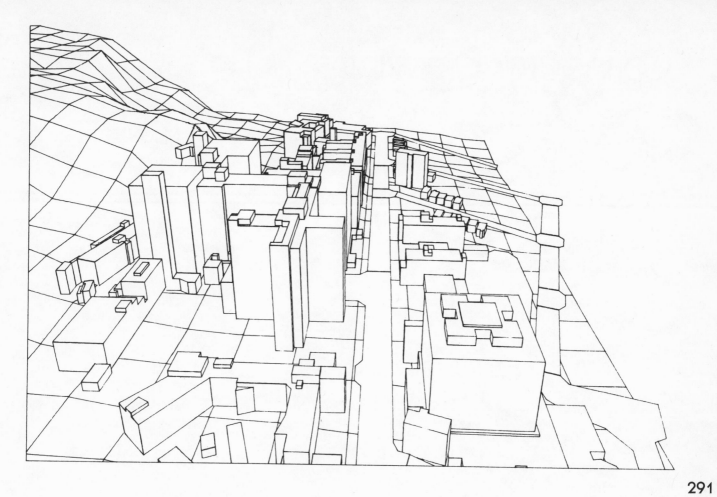

291

COMPUTER PRINTOUT　　　　　　　　　　　　　　　　　　　　ANSHEN AND ALLEN

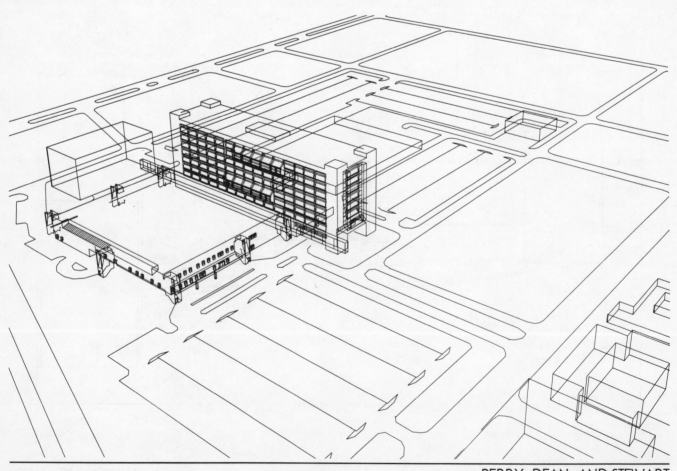

PERRY, DEAN, AND STEWART

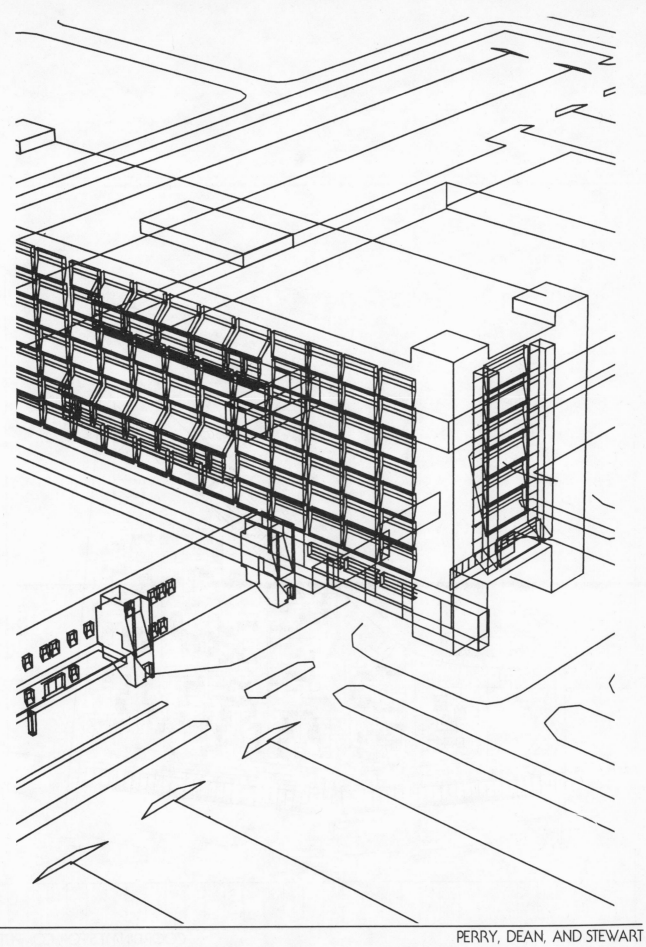

293

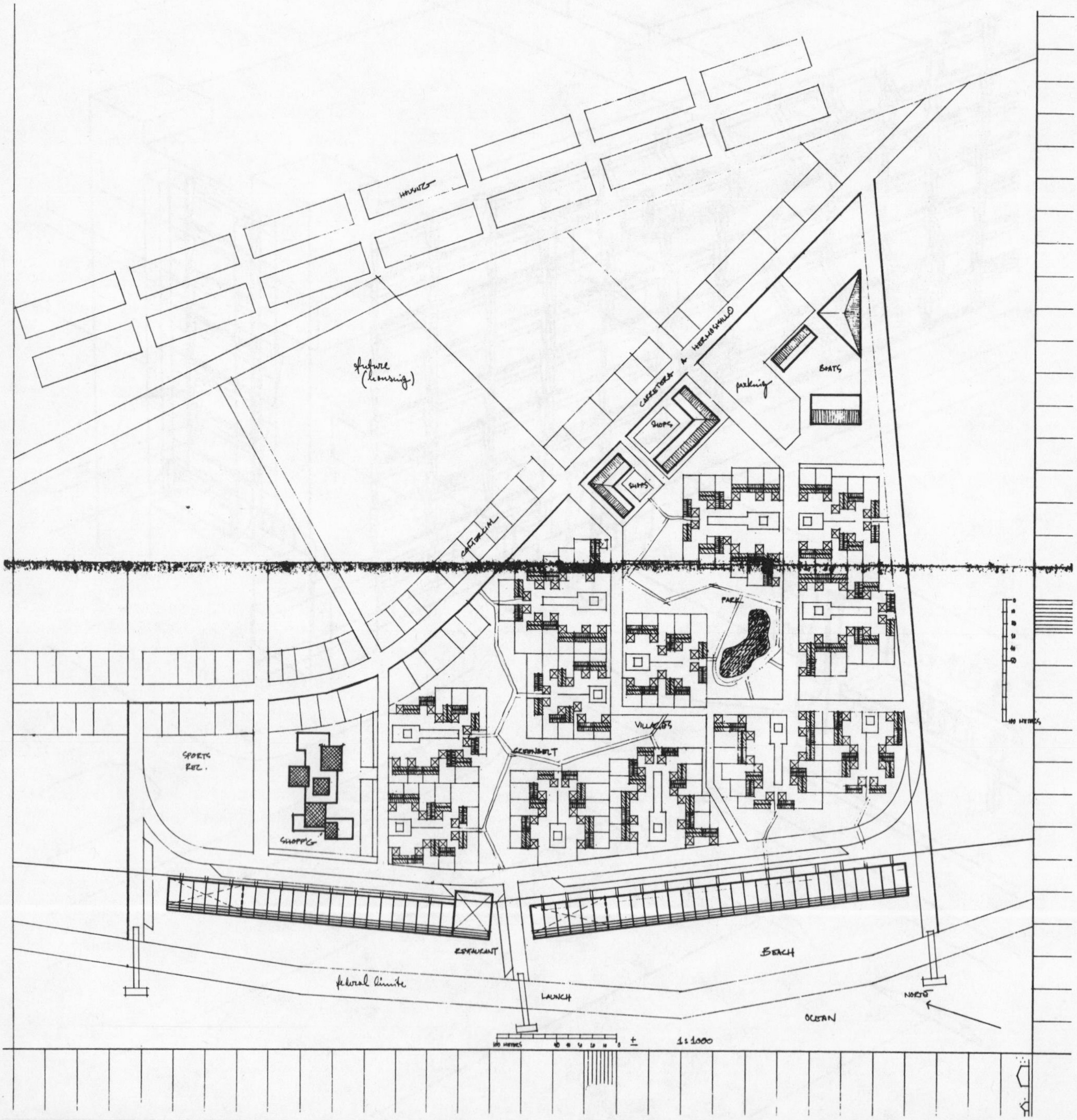

A. M. KEMPER

COORDINATES FOR COMPUTER

A. M. KEMPER

ISOMETRIC FOR COMPUTER PROGRAMMER

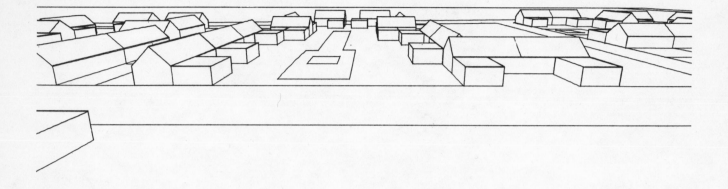

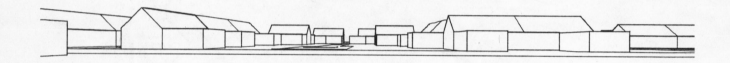

296

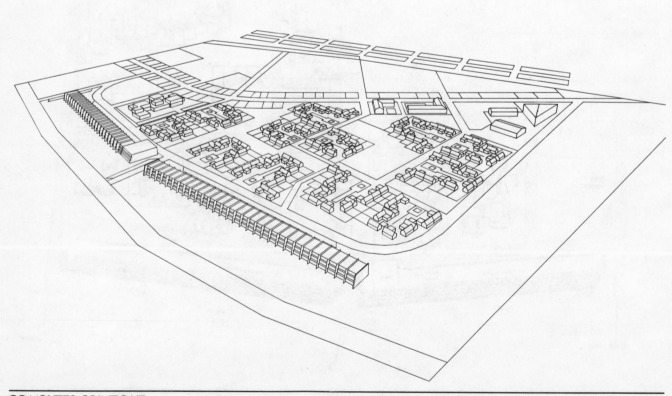

COMPUTER PRINTOUT

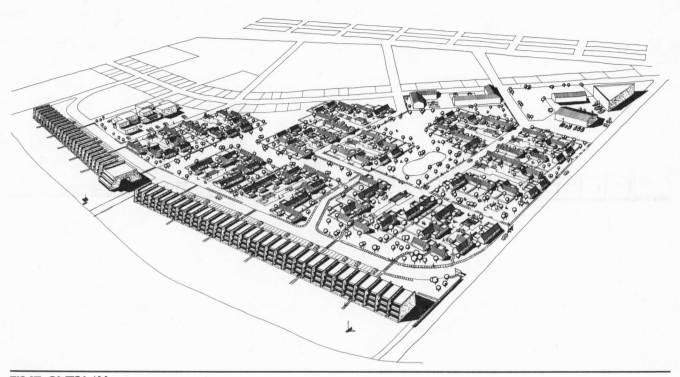

FIRST OVERLAY

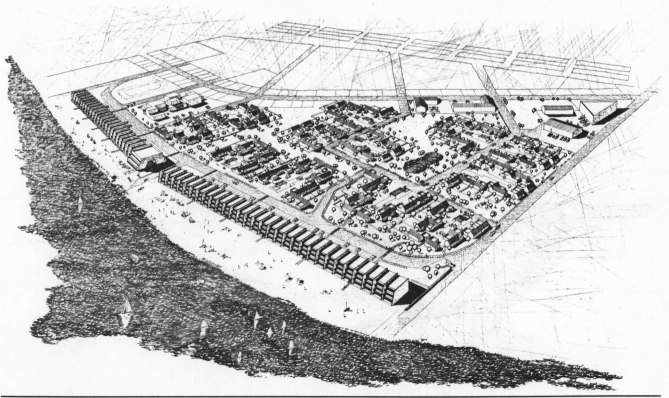

A. M. KEMPER

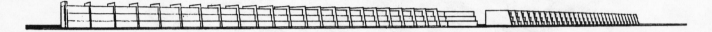

BAHIA KINO-MEX

A. M. KEMPER

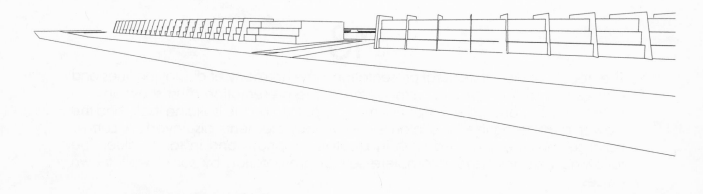

BAHIA KINO - MEXICO

A. M. KEMPER

Complete Sets

18

The beauty of an architectural presentation is the harmony of displaying lines and masses in a skillfully ordered arrangement. The presentation must show unity in both technique and scale. Emphasis must be placed on the building itself, and the viewer must recognize at a glance the various elements displayed. A certain balance must be achieved both in creative emphasis and in tone value. The following examples show complete sets of presentation by some well-known offices.

EARL R. FLANSBURGH AND ASSOCIATES

DESCRIPTION

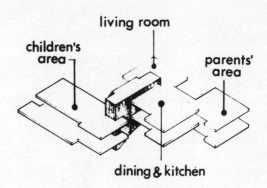

The Problem: Given a beautiful wooded site with a rough, rather small outcropping of granite. The granite outcropping has a beautiful view for 10 miles in two directions and for five miles in the other two. The view looks out through and over the tops of a mixed hard and soft wood forest. Design a house for an athletic family of five. Provide separation of parents and children's area. Three cars will be garaged at the house. If the rock is used for the house it can only be approached from the east.

The Solution: The granite outcropping offered a magnificent site for the house. But because of its small size, to build the house on top of the rock would destroy the beauty of the rock and create a difficult entrance. The most effective way of preserving the natural form of the granite seemed to be to allow the house to float as much as possible over and around the rock. To accomplish this the design was conceived as a group of planes at different levels held together by the strong form of the monitor.

Each major view from the house is different. The breakfast room - kitchen area looks out over the woods approximately 25 feet above the drive way. The children's bedrooms look into the forest. The Monitor passageway and the south side of the dining room look over a handsome knuckle in the rock, through a few dwarf trees and between two wings of the house into the tree tops. The living room and master bedroom look into or through the top most branches of the trees depending on the season. The dressing room views the world through a few hearty trees struggling to grow on top of the rock.

To provide for the time when the children are away at school or have left home the children's area can be isolated simply from the rest of the house.

Because of the family's varied interests a generous amount of storage has been distributed throughout the house.

Cantilevered decks are provided for outside enjoyment of the natural beauty. Also a sheltered deck is available for sitting on windy days and outside cooking with an exterior hearth from the fireplace.

302

Materials:

Foundation: Dark Concrete; Frame: wood, simple span construction; Siding: Rough unplaned pine; Facing: smooth pine; Fins: Smooth Duraply; Decks: Stained Pine; Roof: Tar and Gravel; Sliding doors: Stock Aluminum.

Reasons: Rough texture of wood siding is designed to contrast with smooth facia and fins. Dark concrete foundation designed to emphasize the floating nature of the house over and around the rock. Although a complicated series of planes, simple framing will give economy in construction.

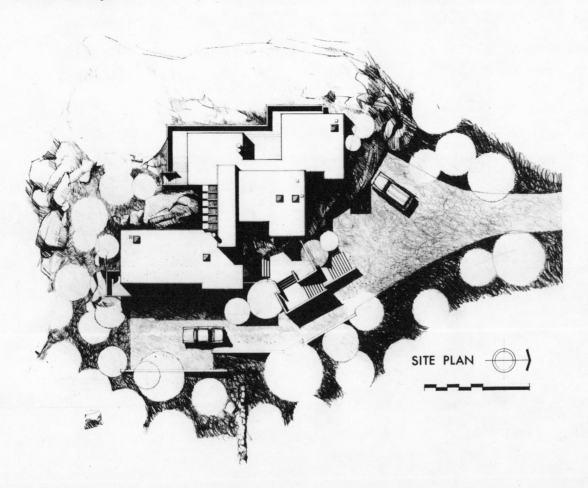

SITE PLAN

PLAN—MAIN LEVEL

0 5 10 15   25ft.

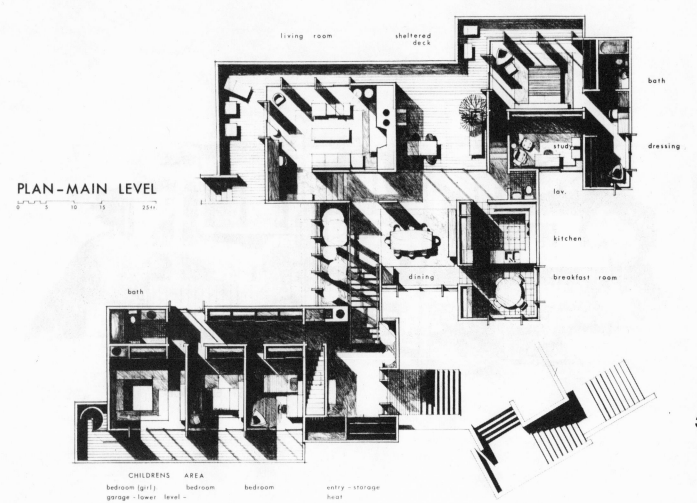

PARENTS AREA
master bedroom

living room   sheltered
deck

bath

study   dressing

lav.

kitchen

dining   breakfast room

bath

CHILDRENS AREA
bedroom (girl).   bedroom   bedroom   entry - storage
garage - lower level -   heat

303

ENTRANCE ELEVATION

EAST ELEVATION

304

TRANSVERSE SECTION

SECTION THROUGH MONITOR

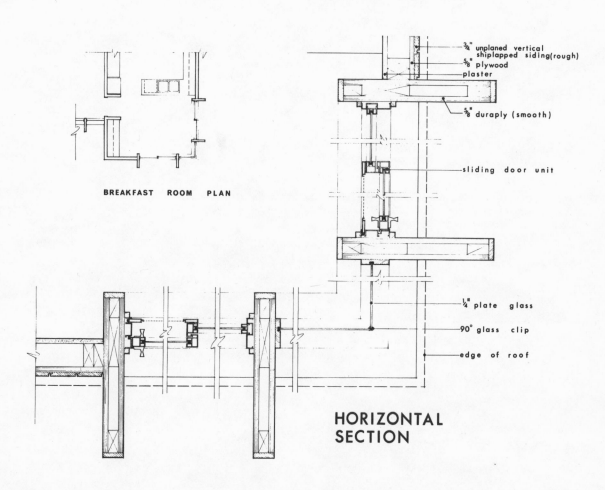

BREAKFAST ROOM PLAN

¾" unplaned vertical
shiplapped siding(rough)
⅝" plywood
plaster

⅝" duraply (smooth)

sliding door unit

¼" plate glass

90° glass clip

edge of roof

HORIZONTAL
SECTION

A. QUINCY JONES, FAIA

307

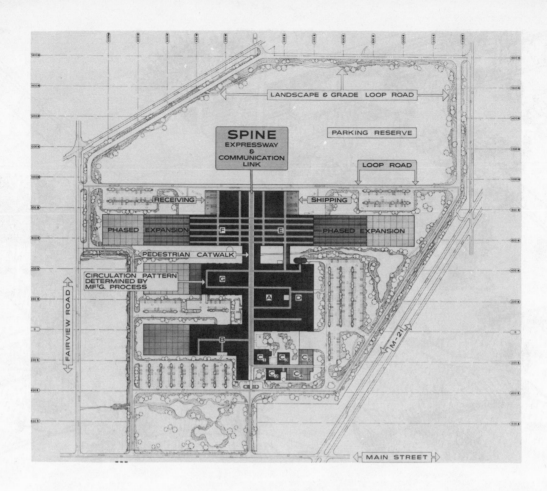

308

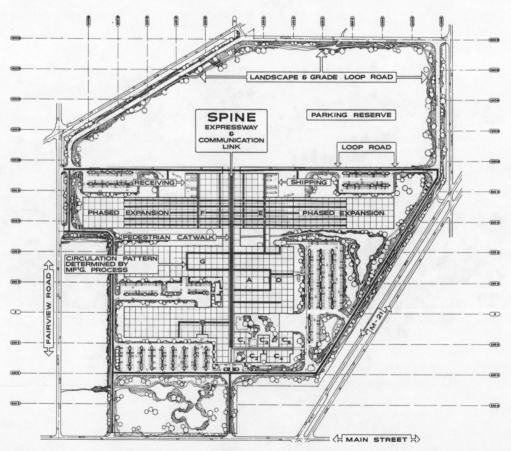

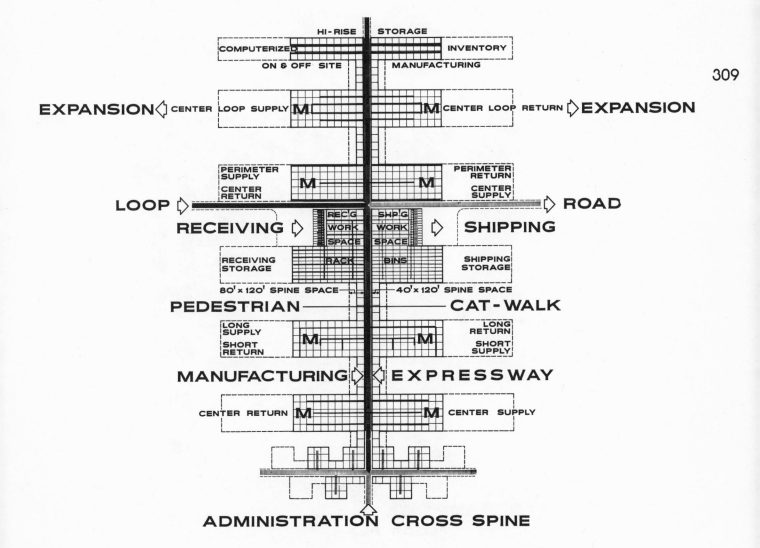

309

ADMINISTRATION CROSS SPINE

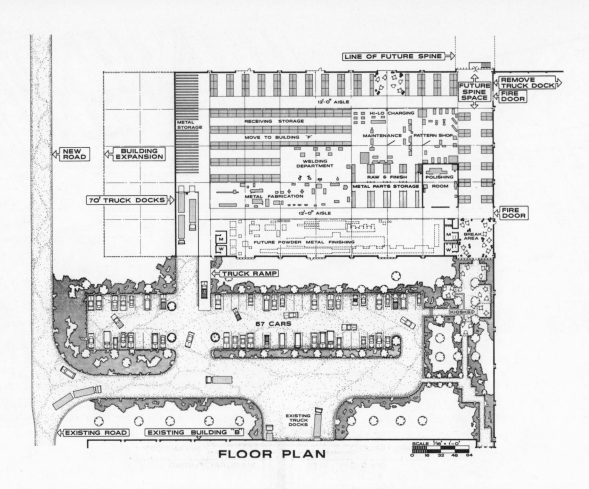

FLOOR PLAN

310

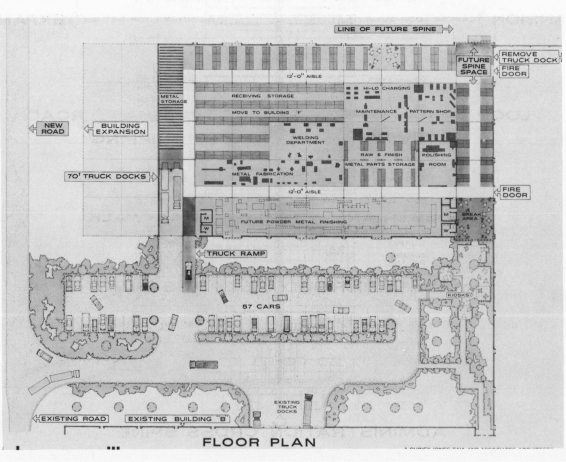

FLOOR PLAN

311

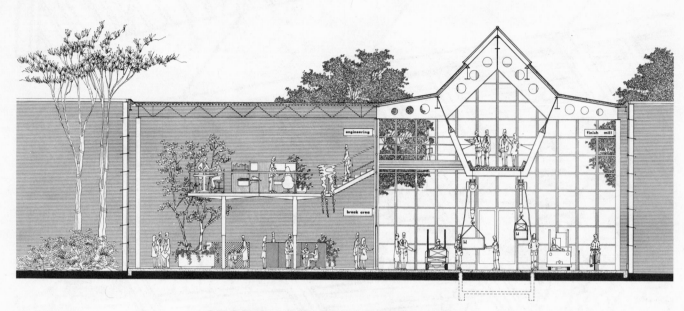

**SECTION AT SPACE BETWEEN
MANUFACTURING BUILDINGS
SPINE CONCEPT**

312

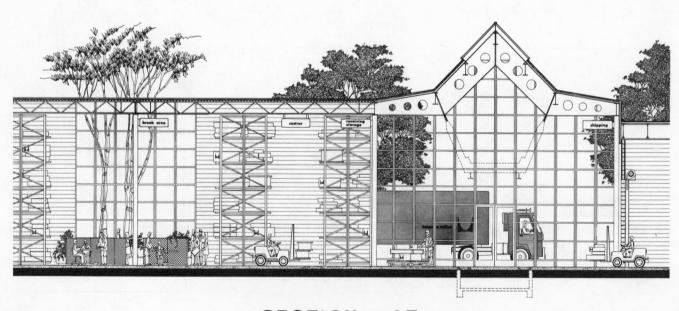

**SECTION AT
MANUFACTURING BUILDINGS
SPINE CONCEPT**

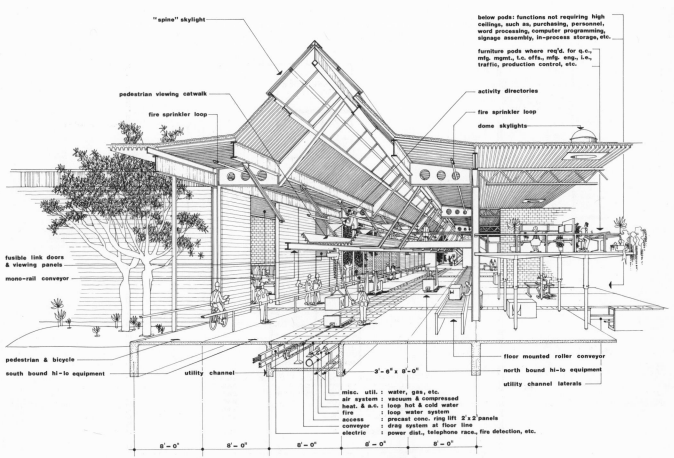

"spine" skylight

below pods: functions not requiring high ceilings, such as, purchasing, personnel, word processing, computer programming, signage assembly, in-process storage, etc.

furniture pods where req'd. for q.c., mfg. mgmt., t.c. offs., mfg. eng., i.e., traffic, production control, etc.

pedestrian viewing catwalk

activity directories

fire sprinkler loop

fire sprinkler loop

dome skylights

fusible link doors & viewing panels

mono-rail conveyor

pedestrian & bicycle

south bound hi-lo equipment

utility channel

floor mounted roller conveyor

north bound hi-lo equipment

utility channel laterals

3'-6" x 8'-0"

misc. util. : water, gas, etc.
air system : vacuum & compressed
heat. & a.c. : loop hot & cold water
fire : loop water system
access : precast conc. ring lift 2' x 2' panels
conveyor : drag system at floor line
electric : power dist., telephone race., fire detection, etc.

8'-0"   8'-0"   8'-0"   8'-0"   8'-0"

SPINE FUNCTIONS

314

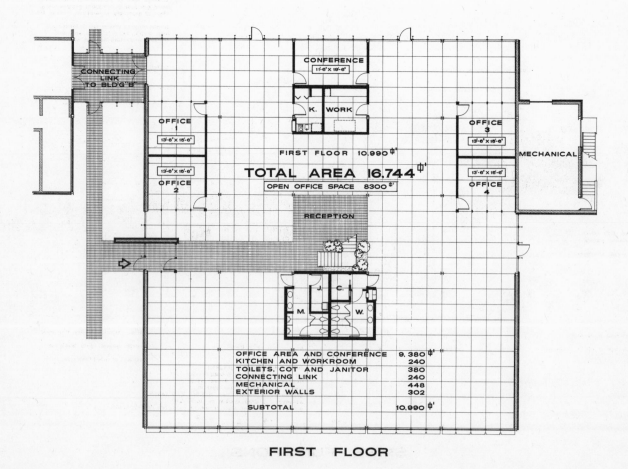

CONNECTING
LINK
TO BLDG 'B'

CONFERENCE
11'-6" X 19'-6"

K. WORK

OFFICE
1
13'-6" X 15'-6"

13'-6" X 15'-6"
OFFICE
2

OFFICE
3
13'-6" X 15'-6"

MECHANICAL

13'-6" X 15'-6"
OFFICE
4

FIRST FLOOR 10,990 □'

TOTAL AREA 16,744 □'

OPEN OFFICE SPACE 8300 □'

RECEPTION

J. C.

M. W.

OFFICE AREA AND CONFERENCE   9,380 □'
KITCHEN AND WORKROOM   240
TOILETS, COT AND JANITOR   380
CONNECTING LINK   240
MECHANICAL   448
EXTERIOR WALLS   302

SUBTOTAL   10,990 □'

FIRST FLOOR

SECTION LOOKING NORTH

315

SOUTH ELEVATION

ROOF FOG SPRAY

AIR CONDITIONING SUPPLY   ACOUSTIC PANELS   LIGHTING

board room

international

SOUTH SIDE NOON SUN

SUMMER   68°-30'
100 % SHADE
0 % SUN

SPRING & FALL   46°-0'
31 1/4 % SHADE
68 3/4 % SUN

ACOUSTIC PANELS   LIGHTING

AIR CONDITIONING SUPPLY

SLOPING BALCONY - HERMAN MILLER ACOUSTIC PANELS

WINTER   21°-0'
15 % SHADE
85 % SUN

conference

customer service

ao 2

break area

ACOUSTIC WALL PANELS

WARM AIR AT GLASS

RADIANT AT PERIMETER

HOT AIR

HOT AIR

316

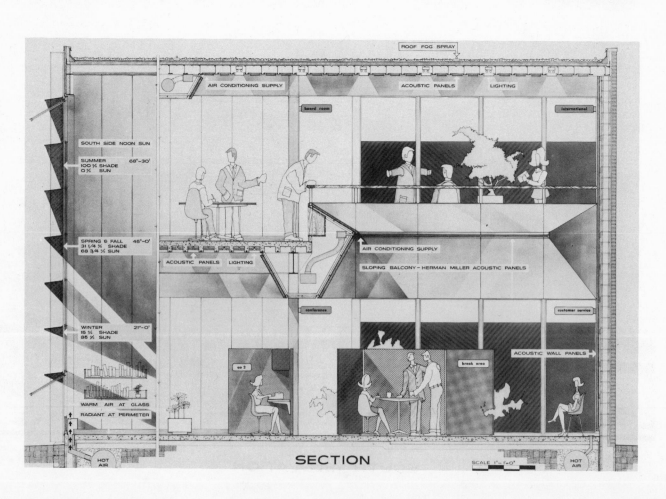

SECTION

SCALE 1"=1'-0"

ANSHEN AND ALLEN

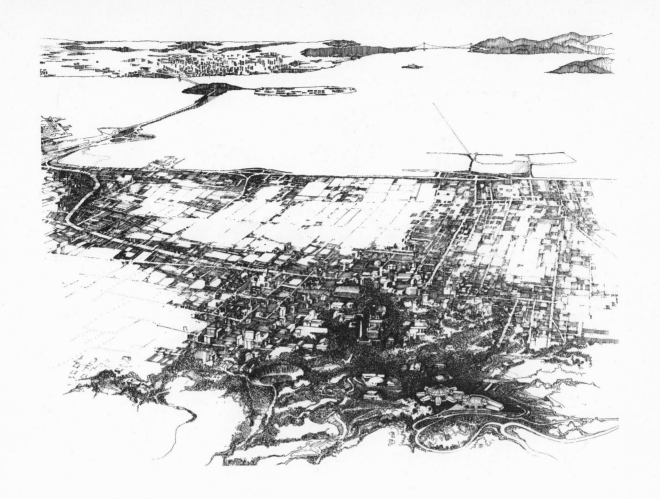

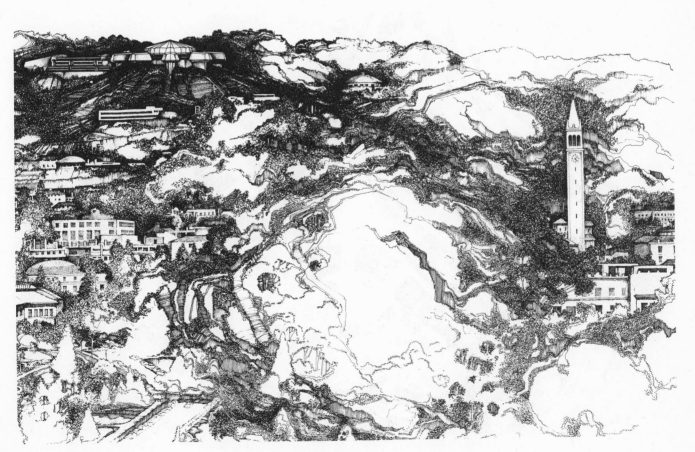

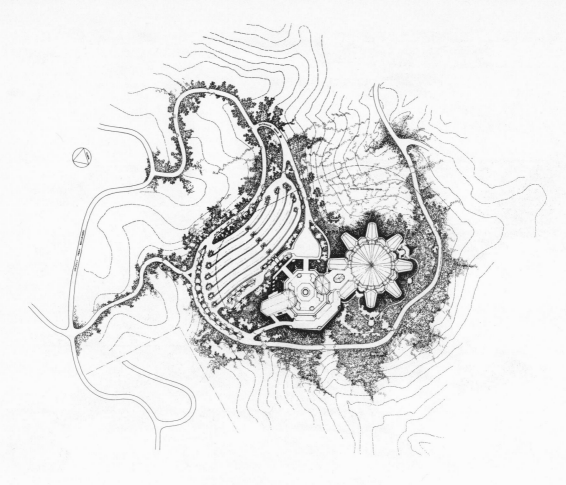

320

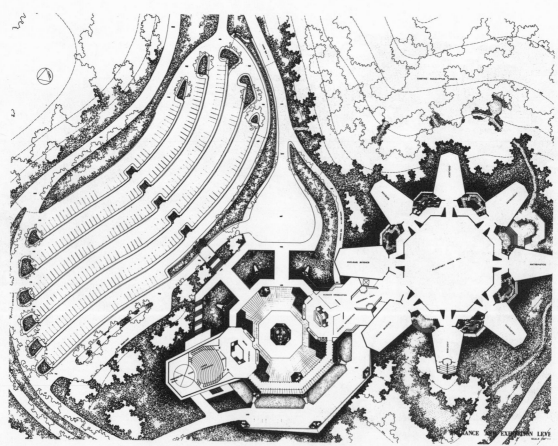

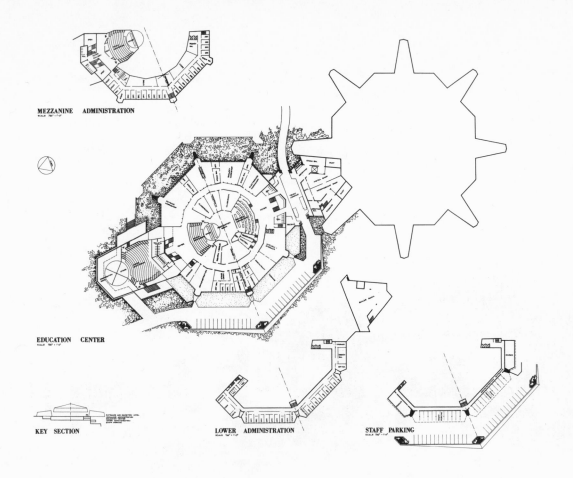

MEZZANINE ADMINISTRATION
SCALE 1/16" = 1'-0"

EDUCATION CENTER
SCALE 1/16" = 1'-0"

KEY SECTION

LOWER ADMINISTRATION
SCALE 1/16" = 1'-0"

STAFF PARKING
SCALE 1/16" = 1'-0"

321

WEST ELEVATION
SCALE 1/16" = 1'-0"

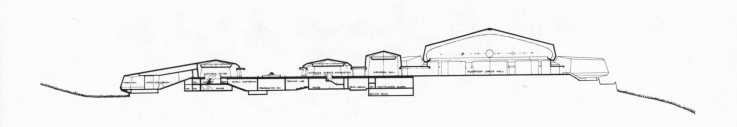

HUGH STUBBINS AND ASSOCIATES

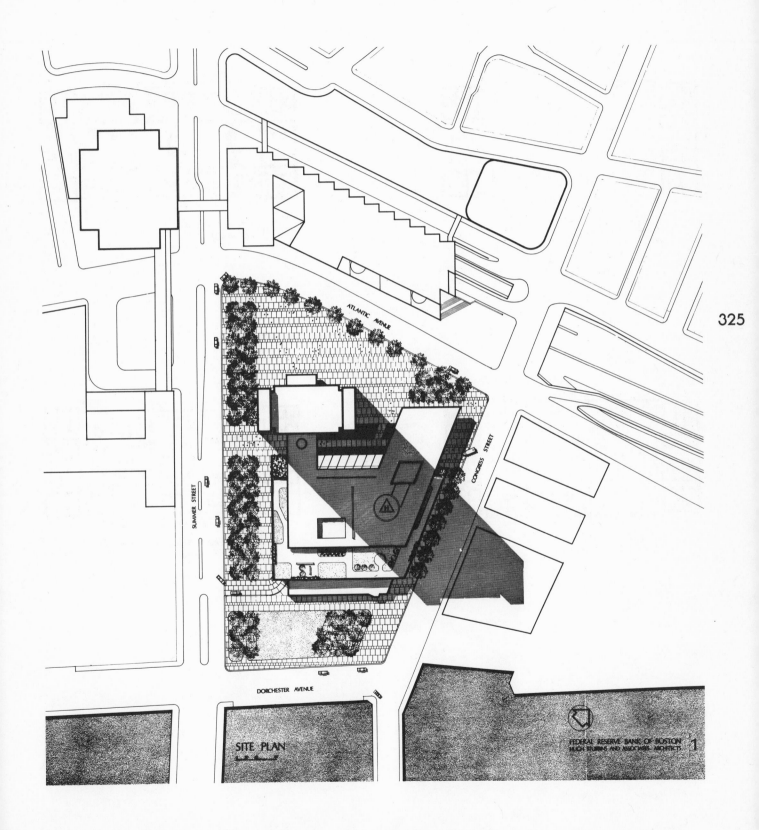

325

ATLANTIC AVENUE

SUMMER STREET

CONGRESS STREET

DORCHESTER AVENUE

SITE PLAN

FEDERAL RESERVE BANK OF BOSTON
HUGH STUBBINS AND ASSOCIATES · ARCHITECTS

1

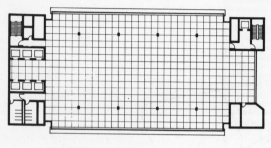

TYPICAL FLOOR PLAN
HIGH RISE ELEVATOR BANK

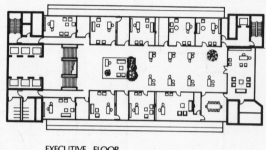

EXECUTIVE FLOOR
34th FLOOR

326

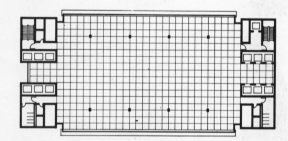

TYPICAL FLOOR PLAN
LOW RISE ELEVATOR BANK

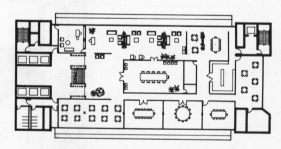

BOARD ROOM / EXECUTIVE DINING LEVEL
33rd FLOOR

TOWER FLOOR PLANS

0   10   20   40

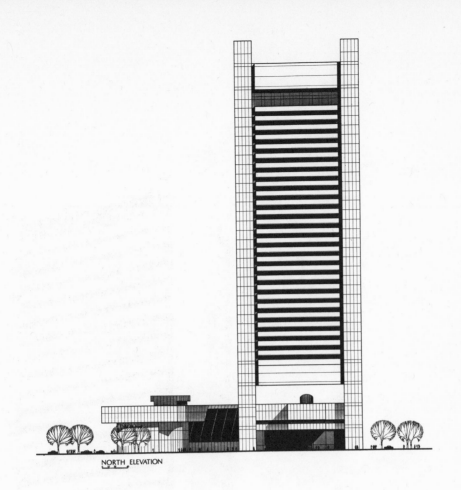

NORTH ELEVATION

EAST ELEVATION

HUYGENS AND TAPPE, INC.

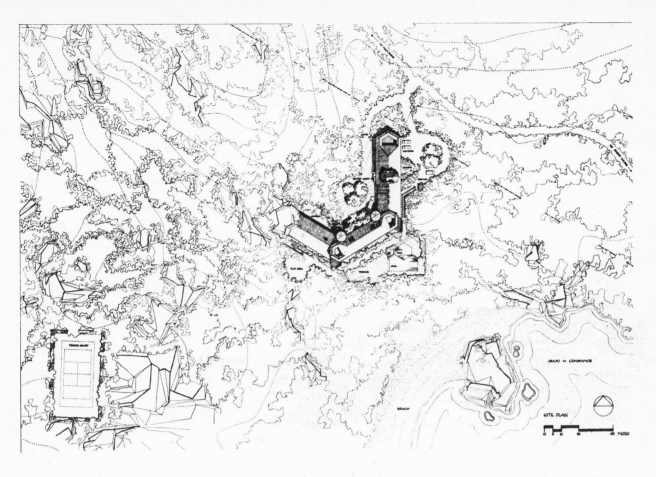

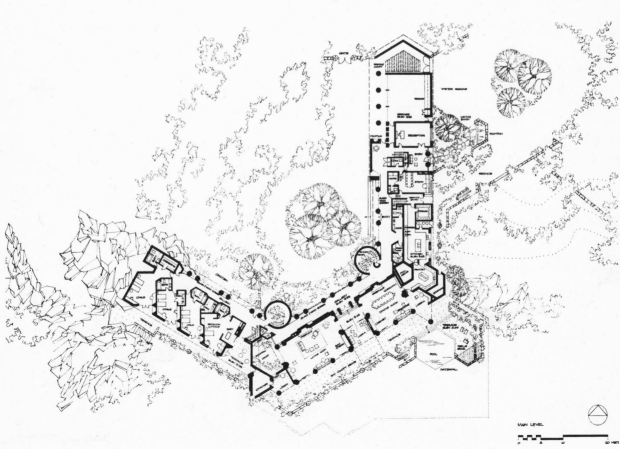

VIEW FROM WEST

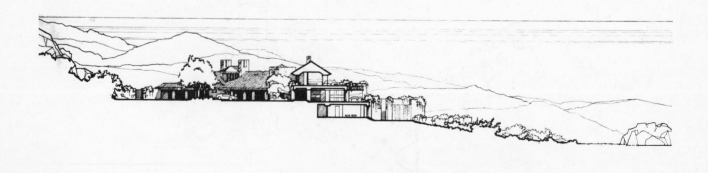

SECTION

0 5 10   30 METERS

333

ENTRANCE COURT

334

VISITOR'S RECEPTION GARDEN

UPPER BREAKFAST

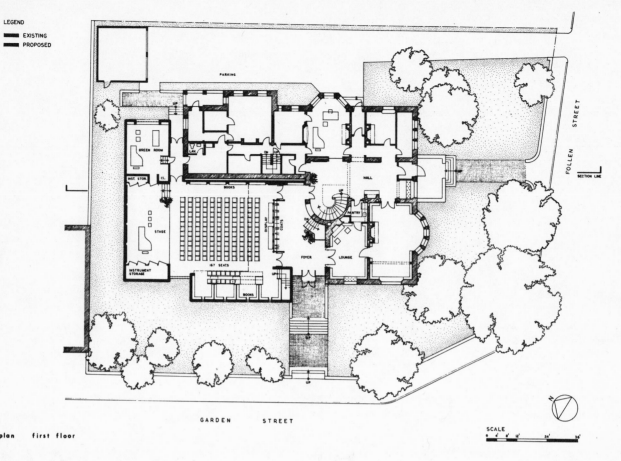

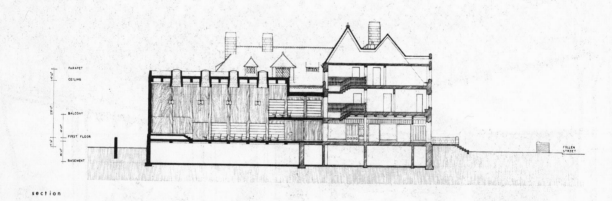

plan   first floor

LEGEND

EXISTING
PROPOSED

PARKING

GREEN ROOM

INST. STOR.   CL.

STAGE

INSTRUMENT STORAGE

BOOKS

167 SEATS

DISPLAY

BOOKS

LAV.

HALL

PANTRY

FOYER

LOUNGE

FOLLEN STREET

SECTION LINE

GARDEN   STREET

SCALE

N

section

PARAPET

CEILING

BALCONY

FIRST FLOOR

BASEMENT

FOLLEN STREET

elevation   garden street

Steve Oles

19

The following section honors Paul Stevenson Oles. In 1968 and 1972 the Architectural League of New York awarded its annual Birch Burdette Long Memorial Prize for Architectural Rendering to Paul Stevenson Oles. The prize is given for "excellence in composition, facility in technique, and expression of the character of the design illustrated." There is little that I can add to this commendation; the following pages testify to a master's skills.

338

RICHARD MEIER AND ASSOCIATES

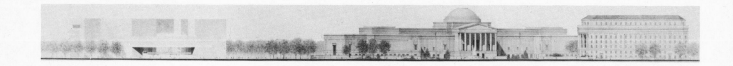

I. M. PEI AND PARTNERS

JOHN CARL WARNECKE AND ASSOCIATES

TAC 341

PRENTICE

Shepley, Bulfinch, Richardson, and Abbott

20

I am very proud to present to you, the reader, the work of one of the nation's few long-established practices. The firm of Shepley, Bulfinch, Richardson, and Abbott is known to every American architect, especially since it has a respected list of architects trained in its offices. As a young architect I could not think of a better way to present a contemporary history of fine architectural drawings that represent more than a century of uninterrupted architectural service. In fact the firm is still occupying the same office space they designed in 1889 and is still producing high-quality architectural drawings equal to those of the founder, the late Henry Hobson Richardson.

It would be inappropriate in this book to catalogue and describe all the historical or contemporary achievements of this office. But, the following selection of drawings needs a brief introduction on the changes that have taken place throughout the past century in their office. The drawings speak for themselves and are indeed a delight to look at. Although our profession is going through the most turbulent changes we have ever faced, looking at these drawings of the past and present not only makes me proud to be a member of the profession but also impels me to hope secretly that all the changes facing us will somehow go away.

In 1866 Henry Hobson Richardson, now remembered among the greatest American architects and the precursors of modern design, opened a small office in New York City and founded the practice that has continued uninterrupted to this day. It was a time of frequent disappointment and marred by hostility to his southern background, but after two years and a few commissions (significantly all in Massachusetts), Richardson entered into partnership with Mr. Charles Gambrill, an older and well-established architect, who allowed him to exercise his genius without interference until the partnership was dissolved in 1878. By 1874 the volume of work in New England had prompted such frequent and lengthy visits to the Boston area that Richardson purchased a house in Brookline, Massachusetts, and moved his family there. Although the partnership with Gambrill remained undissolved, and the firm retained its New York office until 1878, Richardson's new home gave him de facto independence and cemented the strong relationship with New England that the firm has enjoyed ever since. For this reason 1874 is remembered as the date of its establishment in Boston, a date perhaps more significant than that of the founding of Richardson's first small New York office eight years previously.

SHEPLEY, RUTAN AND COOLIDGE

Henry Hobson Richardson died suddenly and prematurely on April 27, 1886, at the very apex of his architectural career. He was but 47 years old and left behind him a large variety of commissions and ripening negotiations, including about 25 projects already under way, some of considerable magnitude. The burden of carrying on his work fell to a triumvirate of younger men, the foremost of whom, George Foster Shepley, a promising designer and trusted aide, was only 26 years of age. Associated with Shepley was Charles Allerton Coolidge, another young designer of 28, and the firm's engineer, Charles H. Rutan, who, at 35, was the oldest of the three. It seems fair to say that this was the firm's most crucial hour, for if these men had proved unequal to the task, a truly staggering one for so young a team, the firm, like so many firms built on the genius of a great architect, would have simply sunk into oblivion.

In 1888 the design of Stanford University in Palo Alto, California, was a vital and successful chapter in the firm's history, and the yellow limestone buildings, with their red tile roofs and arcaded courtyards, preserve much of their original appearance to this day.

In 1889 the firm introduced the skyscraper to Boston by designing the Ames Building, a 14-story bearing wall structure that, though not yet employing the steel frame that was shortly to revolutionize high-rise construction, brought stonemasonry to unprecedented heights and pioneered the concept of the elevator-centered office tower. It is perhaps indicative of the quality of its architecture that the firm's offices are located in this building to this day, more than 80 years after its last stone was laid in place.

344

COURT STREET ELEVATION

1889 WORKING DRAWING BY STAFF

1891 D. A. GREGG

1909 D. A. GREGG

346

1915 HERMAN VOSS

COOLIDGE AND SHATTUCK

Like H. H. Richardson himself, George Foster Shepley was not long-lived, dying in 1903 and leaving the fortunes of the firm in the capable hands of his partners. Mr. Rutan died in 1915, leaving only Charles A. Coolidge, who admitted to partnership George Shattuck, a long-standing employee and M.I.T. graduate. In the following year the Chicago office achieved virtual independence as Coolidge and Hodgon. The Boston firm, under its new name Coolidge and Shattuck, continued to dominate the design of medical schools, first erecting the Rockefeller Center for Medical Research in New York, then a large medical school for Western Reserve University in Cleveland, and, most important, the Peking Union Medical Center, also commissioned by the Rockefeller Foundation. In 1923 the firm began work on the Vanderbilt University medical complex and completed it two years later under the name of Coolidge, Shepley, Bulfinch and Abbott. The history of this period should perhaps begin with a few words about Harvard University, a constant and prolific client, from the building of Sever Hall in 1878 to the present day. At Harvard all facets of the firm's stylistic history are represented, and none more forcefully than the Georgian idiom that Coolidge, Shepley, Bulfinch and Abbott brought to a new level of achievement with the design of the seven Harkness Houses. Dunster House, most prominent of these, occupies a difficult triangular site and is now flanked by Leverett Towers and Mather, its high-rise, present-day successors. From Anderson Bridge to Mather, the entire great bend in the Charles River is lined with a solid wall of the firm's brick buildings, punctuated by the towers of its contemporary houses, and accented by the cupolas and spires of the older houses and of the Memorial Church in the Yard beyond (1933).

348 HERMAN VOSS

D. A. GREGG

1917 HERMAN VOSS

349

1925 HERMAN VOSS

COOLIDGE, SHEPLEY, BULFINCH AND ABBOTT

Charles Allerton Coolidge died in 1936, leaving his work in the very capable hands of Henry Richardson Shepley, architect of the New York Hospital and the supreme driving force of the firm for the next quarter of a century. It was under Mr. Shepley's firm guidance that Coolidge, Shepley, Bulfinch and Abbott, and later Shepley, Bulfinch, Richardson and Abbott, continued to prosper and grow to its present size and prominence. The firm not only continued to practice in its many established specializations but also continued to diversify, completing projects such as the U.S. Parcel Post Building in Boston, the progressive BB Chemical Plant of 1938, and Logan International Airport (1945–1953). The planning of a great airport was a fitting continuation to the firm's railroad station work, which, after 58 of these structures had been built, declined with the fortunes of the railroads themselves.

350

1872 HENRY R. SHEPLEY

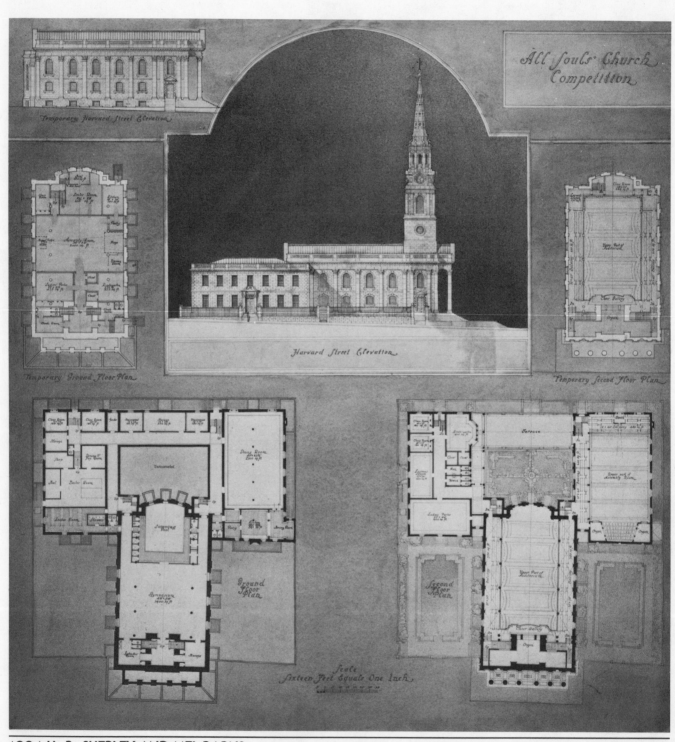

352

1924 H. R. SHEPLEY AND MEL BARNS

Sixteenth Street Elevation
scale sixteen feet equals one inch

All Souls'
Church
Competition

1924 H. R. SHEPLEY

354 1930

1930 CONSTANTIN A. PERTZOFF

1932 CONSTANTIN A. PERTZOFF

356

1932 CONSTANTIN A. PERTZOFF

·HOUSE·3·HARVARD·UNIVERSITY·—·VIEW·FROM·MEMORIAL·DRIVE·

1932 CONSTANTIN A. PERTZOFF

358

1934 MARCEL SHAPPEY

1934 MARCEL SHAPPEY 359

SECTION

COMPETITION FOR A BUILDING FOR THE FEDERAL RESERVE BOARD

JAMES FORD CLAPP, JR. & HOEDTKE

1940 HERMAN VOSS

1943 HERMAN VOSS

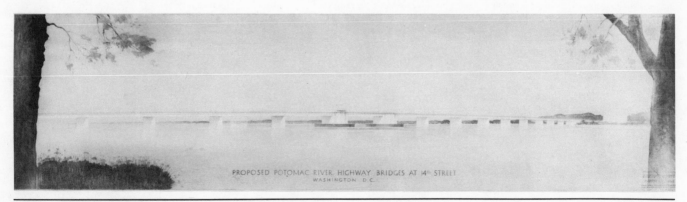

PROPOSED POTOMAC RIVER HIGHWAY BRIDGES AT 14th STREET
WASHINGTON D.C.

1944 HERMAN VOSS

SHEPLEY, BULFINCH, RICHARDSON AND ABBOTT

In 1952 another change in the firm's name took place, the name of Joseph Priestley Richardson being substituted for that of C. A. Coolidge, then dead 16 years. So it was that, with the death of Henry Richardson Shepley in 1962 (whose son, Hugh Shepley, is a present partner), a Richardson once more assumed the senior partnership, almost a century after his illustrious grandfather had opened his first modest architectural office in New York City. Of the firm's most recent endeavors, we need only say that it has continued to be tremendously active in all its traditional areas of competence and has never lacked the flexibility and talent to diversify when the opportunity presented itself. In 1973 the American Institute of Architects chose Shepley, Bulfinch, Richardson and Abbott to receive its Architectural Firm Award, an honor shared only by nine other firms in history. In bestowing the award, the Jury on Institute Honors noted that the firm had "contributed the best at all times" during its first century of practice. It enters its second century of practice fully prepared to face the challenges that lie ahead.

362

1956 HERMAN VOSS

1957 HELMUT JACOBY

1957 HELMUT JACOBY

1960 HARRY WIJK

366

1961 HARRY WIJK

1961 HARRY WIJK

1963 HELMUT JACOBY

SECTION

1. GREAT HALL
2. MAZE
3. TICKET BOOTH
4. BULL PEN
5. ELEVATOR
6. TRAMWAY CAR BOARDING
7. TRAMWAY CAR
8. CONTROL ROOM
9. TRAMWAY EXIT
10. UPPER MACHINE ROOM
11. COUNTERWEIGHTS
12. HAUL ROPE SHAFT
13. MACHINE ROOM
14. MACHINE VIEWING GALLERY
15. SKI RENTAL
16. MANAGER'S OFFICE

368   1969 RAY WARBUTON

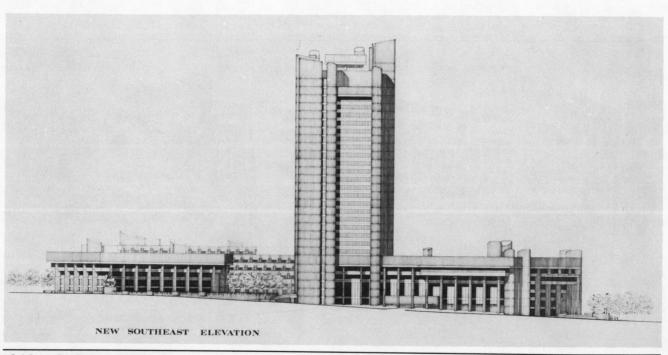

NEW SOUTHEAST ELEVATION

1969 LLOYD P. ACTON, JR.

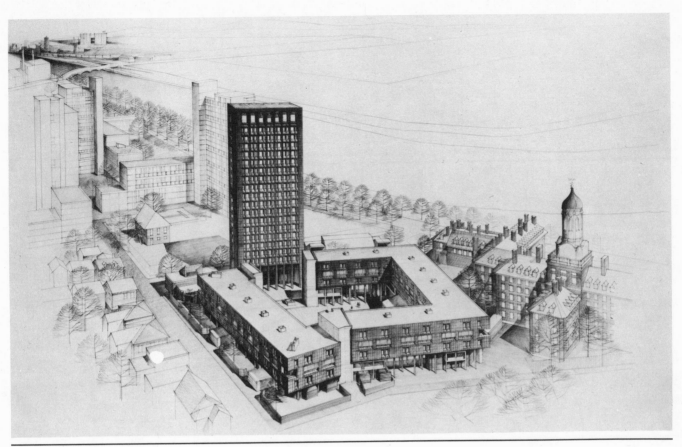

369

1969 PAUL SUN

1970 PAUL SUN

1972 R. K. WARBURTON

372 1971 PAUL SUN

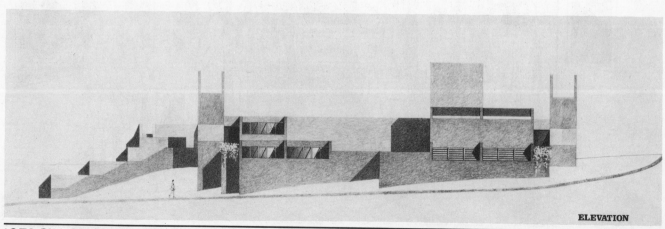

ELEVATION

1973 BILL BRICKEN

1974 PAUL SUN

Index of Renderers

375

376

Index of Offices

378

379

380